Lord, these are the first words a casual reader's eyes will light upon.

In this moment—grab him, God.

Spin him around, knock him off his feet, flatten him, pin him.

Hold him there for 170 pages, on his back.

Then there's no place to look but up, Father. One hundred seventy pages: that may be the longest time he's thought about worship, ever.

Oh-oh, he heard the word "worship" and he's wiggling. Pin him good, Lord.

Pin him until he feels desperately impotent. You know how we are about worship, God—quick to clothe ourselves, quick to make motions, quick to say words. . . . Stuff your almighty fist in his mouth, O Most High. Hold your omnipotent knee on his chest.

He's wonderfully quiet. Oh, God, he's turning blue. You've seen it: you're breathing your holy breath into him. . . .

Now he's ready to read.

Alleluia.

UP WITH WORSHIP

How to Quit Playing Church

ANNE ORTLUND

Regal Books

Rights for publishing this book in other languages are contracted by Gospel Literature International (GLINT) foundation. GLINT also provides technical help for the adaptation, translation, and publishing of Bible study resources and books in scores of languages worldwide. For further information, contact GLINT, Post Office Box 6688, Ventura, California 93006, U.S.A., or the publisher.

Published by Regal Books
A Division of GL Publications
Ventura, California 93006
Printed in U.S.A.

Library of Congress Cataloging in Publication Data

   Ortlund, Anne.
     Up with worship.

     1. Public worship.   I. Title.
   BV15.077 1982   264   82-15063
   ISBN 0-8307-0867-7

3 4 5 6 7 8 9 10 11 12 13 14 15/91 90 89 88 87 86

CONTENTS

Dedicated to my pastor,
a godly man whose life and words
constantly urge me to Christ.
I'm so lucky—
I'm even married to him.

Part One
LET'S TALK ABOUT CHURCH

IS YOUR CHURCH FOR REAL?

Settle down for a really honest yes or no

When I was little we used to play church. We'd get the chairs into rows, fight over who'd be preacher, vigorously lead the hymn singing, and generally have a great carnal time.

The aggressive kids naturally wanted to be up front, directing or preaching. The quieter ones were content to sit and be entertained by the up-fronters.

Occasionally we'd get mesmerized by a true sensationalistic crowd-swayer—like the girl who said, "Boo! I'm the Holy Ghost!" But in general, if the up-fronters were pretty good they could hold their audience quite a while. If they weren't so good, eventually the kids would drift off to play something else—like jump rope or jacks.

Now that generation has grown up, but most of them haven't changed too much. Every Sunday they still play church. They line up in rows for the entertainment. If it's pretty good, their church may grow. If it's not too hot, eventually they'll drift off to play something else—like yachting or wife swapping.

Not often do churchgoers find themselves in the Presence!

But when they do—

All is changed. They may destroy their idols, as in Genesis 35:2.

They may, as a group, promise to obey all of God's Word, as in Exodus 24:7.

They may have a great musical time, as in 2 Chronicles 5:11-14.

They may be moved to weeping, as in Nehemiah 8:9.

They may just have a wonderful "ball" enjoying God! In Nehemiah 8:6 they said, "Amen," lifted their hands toward heaven and then bowed and worshiped with their faces toward the ground.

In any case, they are moved to *move*! Repent—weep—rejoice—*something*! When God is present in power, if the people don't respond the very stones will.

———————————

I don't know about you. If you've never been in church when God was obviously present, may this book make you so thirsty for that to happen, you'll be absolutely cotton-mouthed.

If you have—do you remember? Stop and recall. Oh, holy, glorious, sweaty-palms time! If you were the leader, you wondered when—how—if you should put a lid on this bubbling pot!

———————————

One thing is sure: you knew, "Oh, God, this is what I was made for. This is stretching and rewarding and fulfilling, down deep in my bones. This is Eternity Business. I'm being caught up into the Important."

This is—breaking into glory!

———————————

After that you will never again be satisfied to just play church.

2
ON THE STREETS WHERE WE HAVE LIVED

By now we must be qualified to write this book

Ray and I have ministered for over thirty years in four pastorates. (Is it wrong for a wife to state it like that? I've had a subordinate role, but I've been there!) We've been in an old country church, a young suburban one, a downtown city one, and one that's new, experimental, and "beachy." We've been in mainline denominations and independent fellowships. We've worked with budgets of thirty thousand or millions, and with congregations from 100 to thirty-four hundred. We've pastored formal and informal churches, traditional and untraditional. We've loved them all.

During the last dozen years, God has also commissioned us to an umbrella ministry of conferences to churches, pastors, missionaries, and denominations all over the world. Under the auspices of Renewal Ministries, we've spoken to several of the largest Southern Baptist churches in the world; to Episcopal churches who sang their chants and waved incense; to Mennonite groups in their bonnets and plain clothes; to Free Methodists and United Methodists and "G.A.R.B.s" and Presbyterians; to charismatic churches and anti-charismatic. Ray has preached in lace beside an enormous crucifix in Lutheran Germany; he's shed his wolfskin long enough to preach beside a potbellied stove to seven hundred Eskimos. He's served shorter pastorates in Kabul, Afghanistan, and suburban London. We've loved them all and wished they loved each other!

We've seen much blessing, and sometimes outright renewal and revival. Uppermost in our speaking we stress God Himself as "Priority One"! We find that His people everywhere, of whatever background, are hungry to confront Him meaningfully when they gather together.

That's what *Up with Worship* is all about.

What happens when *you* gather with fellow believers? What happens in *your* church?

For us, we say, "What is the Holy Spirit doing today? Let's do *that*. Where is He going today? Let's go *there*. What can we do—*in this day*—to bring God and His people truly together?"

In this day!

A living church (small or large, traditional or not) is a contemporary one; it isn't trying to be twenty years ahead—strained and strange.

It isn't content to be twenty years behind—musty and dusty.

A living church gathers up all of its age groups and says, "Come! In this precious, unique, 'now' time, let's all together go hard after God!"

WORSHIPING IN THE NOW

You've got to fit into this particular slice of God's eternity

Let me describe what Pentecost *wasn't* like, all right?

Picture all those believers meeting together; suddenly there's the sound of a mighty rushing wind and it fills all the house where they're sitting.

"Great! This is wonderful!" they cry. "Quick! Shut the windows! Let's capture this glorious wind forever!"

So twenty, thirty years later, there they sit—faces flushed, eyes glazed, remembering the day God came—and determined to keep everything exactly as it was then.

My friend, the wind is a *wind*. You can't trap it, you just have to go with it. Thus it is with the Holy Spirit!

Past successes can completely undo you, Christian, and undo your church too. God blessed something so wonderfully a while back; it was so beautiful; so you work at it, you fan it, you wear out the saints trying to revive it. But, friend, God has gone on to something else—and you don't even know it!

Forget yesterday; today is God's precious gift. His name is "I AM." He is forever contemporary.

Christians who stay with Him are the same—they're happy, "now" people. Churches who stay with Him are happy, "now" churches. "The old has gone, the new has come!" (2 Cor. 5:17). "Forgetting the past, they press on to what lies ahead" (Phil. 3:13, paraphrase).

They stay current because God is current, and they're with Him! They have a built-in sloughing-off process, by which the worn-out gets eliminated.

————————

How is it with you, Christian? Have you taken a day off lately to get alone with God and fast and pray and say, "What in my life needs to go? What has 'had it'? What new good thing needs to be strengthened or added?"

How is it with your church? When the Body comes together to worship God, do you ask, "What's gotten dreary? What needs to go? What needs to be freshened, changed? What needs to be added? Where are we as a people? What are our needs? What would be great for God? How can we all together connect with Him—in *this* world—*today*?"

4
WORSHIP SERVICES CAN'T BE SERVED SMORGASBORD

"Let me see: shall I have contemporary or traditional today?"

The game plan for this book is that it deals with the local church, maybe *your* church, in how to bring life out of deadness—in how to make the worship service a happening. So sometimes it talks to pastor, sometimes to organist, sometimes to a person in the pew, sometimes to choir director. But everybody needs to know the philosophy behind what everybody else is doing; so everybody needs to read all of the game plan, right?

One thing we learn about God's dealing with people is that He does it in *togetherness*.

The children of Israel moved *together* across the wilderness. (That wasn't always easy.)

The young, vigorous ones probably wanted to go twice the pace.

The young mothers with babies and toddlers needed to take it easy.

The oldest probably never wanted to move at all.

It took a lot of give and take, a lot of consideration for the condition of the other fellow, a lot of accommodating. But when it was all over, except for those who died along the way, they all got from *here* to *there*—together.

They all obeyed the sight of cloud and fire, the sound of trumpets.

They grumbled and were punished together—but together they also saw waters part, rods bud, and fire come out of heaven.

They knew each other well. They did it all together.

———————

Pastor, in however long a time God gives you with your people—three years, thirty years—you have to get your people from here to there, together. Lead them together. Help them feel *all one*. The pagan deity Janus was two-faced: one face looked forward and the other looked back. A congregation will become two-faced when the conservatives attend the one consistently "straight" service while the "progressives" experiment with the latest in contemporary.

No, no! Put elements of both old and new in whatever the people experience, but pace your people to go forward experiencing everything together.

Some older ones will grumble.

Some younger ones will want to cavort more.

Expect both reactions and help them to be considerate of each other's feelings.

Do you have several morning services? Try to make them identical so that there will be a wide spread of ages in each service. Preach the same sermon each time.

Give them the feeling when it's all over that they grumbled and endured together, but they saw some glory together too. Together they all lost some of the old; together they all gained some of the new; but they all were a Body together—conservatives and progressives struggling to put it together—together!

After all, every car must have both gas and brakes. That's the very way it gets from here to there.

THREE CHEERS FOR STIFF, RIGID ROWS OF PEWS!

Alternatives may become humanistic

This is the age of stress on "relationships." I'm-okay-you're . . . et cetera. Everyone is so lonely—that's why we're reaching out.

We're discovering fellowship and it's great. When we discover worship, it will be greater.

We're discovering "Body life," and that's essential. But we haven't yet gazed too long at the Head. Thank the Lord for small groups! Circles of friends gathered in His name are wonderful. They bring me out of myself to others.

But better than being us-centered is being God-centered. Better than circles is being shoulder to shoulder—whether standing, sitting, kneeling or on our faces. Better than "sharing" is worshiping—aware of one another only in that deep, joyous awareness of being caught up together in God.

Eyes—minds—hearts "front and center"!

People say, "But rows are so impersonal." Exactly!

Jesus took His very dearest friends with Him up the mountain to pray.

But then He withdrew from them a stone's throw.

THE CHURCH SERVICE IS A STAGE PLAY

Who's in the spotlight?

So the people all come together in rows in the church, and they face forward. So what?

Well, it's the same physical setup as a stage play, and everybody knows about *those*. You plunk down in a seat. At H-hour the lights go up, the actors start performing, a prompter offstage whispers cues—and the spectators lean back and evaluate how they do.

But church? NO, NO, NO, NO, NO, NO, NO!

Church is unique. Whether the people in the congregation ever discover it or not, *they* are the actors. The up-front people are the prompters, whispering cues as needed—and God is the Audience, looking on to see how they do. (Kierkegaard said it first. I didn't. But that analogy has really helped me. Maybe it will you.)

Many poor churches don't even know who's supposed to be *doing it*! What lousy, lousy plays they put on! The actors sit around lethargically while the prompters practically exhaust themselves trying to do all their lines for them so the play will still give a lively appearance.

It doesn't.

Nobody is fooled.

Pastor, minister of music, organist, what are you so self-conscious for? Do you think you're in the spotlight? You're not. Quit posturing! Just get down on your knees and ask God to stimulate you and your people together to start performing.

BROKEN BOTTLES

How do you get a congregation going?

Dear up-front people! Are you really burdened about that flock of yours? Do you care? Do you see them as just an impossible bunch?

A while back, Ray preached on Mark 14:3. "Here came Mary," he said, "with her alabaster vase of nard to the dinner where Jesus was. She broke the bottle and poured it on Him."

An alabaster vase—milky white, veined, smooth, precious.

And pure nard inside! Gone forever. According to John 12:3, the whole house became filled with the fragrance.

Some story.

———

Christians file into church on a Sunday morning. One by one by one they march in—like separate alabaster vases.

Contained.

Self-sufficient.

Encased.

Individually complete.

Contents undisclosed.

No perfume emitting at all.

Their vases aren't bad looking. In fact, some of

them are the Beautiful People, and they become Vase-Conscious: conscious of their own vase and of one another's. They're aware of clothes, of personalities, of position in this world—of exteriors.

So before and after church (maybe during) they're apt to talk Vase Talk. *Your ring is darling; what stone is that? Did you hear if Harry got that job? What is Lisa's boy doing for the summer? Is that all your own hair? I may take tennis lessons if George wants to.*

Mary broke her vase.

Broke it?! How shocking. How controversial. Was everybody doing it? Was it a vase-breaking party? No, she just did it all by herself. What happened then? The obvious: all the contents were forever released. She could never hug her precious nard to herself again.

Many bodies who file into church, no doubt, do so because they have Jesus inside of them. Jesus!—precious, exciting, life giving. But most of them keep Him shut up, contained, enclosed all their lives. And the air is full of NOTHING. They come to church and sit—these long rows of cold, beautiful, alabaster vases! Then the cold, beautiful, alabaster vases get up and march out again, silently—or maybe talking their cold alabaster talk—to repeat the ritual week after week, year after year.

Unless they just get too bored and quit.

The need for Christians everywhere (nobody is exempt) is to be broken. The vase has to be smashed! Christians have to let the life out! It will fill the room with sweetness. And the congregation will all be broken shards, mingling together for the first time.*

Of *course* it's awkward and scary to be broken! Of *course* it's easier to keep up that cold alabaster front.

It was costly for Mary too.

When Ray preached on Mark 14:3, I wrote on a card, "Lord, break my strong will, my argumentativeness, my quickness to reach decisions ahead of others and always think I'm right, my desire to have my opinion always considered. I'm sure I'm often obnoxious, Lord—maybe embarrassing to Ray. Forgive me, and help my fervent spirit be converted into just being fervent in loving you, fervent in joy, fervent in peace, et cetera. Lord, break me. Thank you for doing it! Amen."

We see the same truth in other Scriptures. In John 12:24,25 that hard, closed-up seed with precious life inside has to fall into the ground and die before the life can spring up. In 2 Corinthians 4:6,7 the clay vessel has light inside, but who could ever see light through a clay pot? Do you know what happens to a roomful of Christians when all the clay pots get broken at once? What glory! What light!

What is the need as people come together as a congregation? It is for them to be broken together.

"The high and lofty one who inhabits eternity, the Holy One . . ." (How do I get there, Lord?) ". . . says this: I live in that high and holy place where those with contrite, humble spirits dwell; and I

---

*I remember one time when God broke us all together at Wheaton College, one of the students said it was like Orientation Week all over again: they were beginning to get to know one another.

refresh the humble and give new courage to those with repentant hearts" (Isa. 57:15, *TLB*).

———————

The way to up is down!

The Holy One lives among broken people!

Christian, break your vase. Help your brothers and sisters break theirs. Split those exteriors. Have a smashing time. Then life will begin to mingle and flow around you and fill the whole church with the fragrance of Jesus!

When vases get broken, vase-awareness goes. The wealthy tennis player has his arm around the asthmatic stamp collector. The black high-school boy joshes freely with the wheeler-dealer car salesman. Spirits commune with spirits. Interiors and exteriors mingle unselfconsciously, because whole people are talking to whole people.

Your ring is darling; what stone is that? . . . I praise the Lord for the look on your face as you sang that hymn this morning. . . . Did you hear if Harry got that job? I was asking God to encourage him this week, one way or another. . . . What is Lisa's boy doing for the summer? . . . I just have to tell you what I found in Isaiah 6 this morning. . . . You must pray for me; the old temper really flared up yesterday. . . . I appreciate you, sister; thanks for ministering to my daughter this week. You said what I couldn't say. . . .

The nard fills the air. Beautiful! Take a deep breath.

———————

If you know one another as broken people, you're ready to get on with a church service.

8

WHEN LAKE AVENUERS GOT BROKEN

We discovered that God is the God of the desperate

Ray and I had left our congregation at Lake Avenue Church in California five times to minister in far-off places. Each time our own flock prayed around the clock for us, as they did whenever we went. (People signed up for 15-minute prayer periods, night and day, during the period of ministry. They'll never, never know what that support meant to us.) One particular summer they began to show frustration.

Ray had been pastoring the only Christian church in Afghanistan for three months. We came back with stories of how the Holy Spirit had broken through in power in that little struggling church, reviving His people. At the time we didn't know the reason for this special revival, but it was to prepare for persecution to come.

Our people said, "We pray for other people around the clock and they experience revival. Why don't we pray for ourselves?" So in June the dear people prayed around the clock. And what happened was—they just prayed around the clock. Nothing else special. Was God teaching us that He was not a bellboy who would jump every time the buzzer sounded? But for years prayer groups had prayed specifically for revival. Surely He was not turning a deaf ear—?

Again in December the flock prayed continuously as Ray and I saw missionaries in Peru meet the Lord in a fresh way through many hours of tears, joy, confession, repentance, and glory.

This increased frustration for Lake Avenuers.

Ray and I talked to God.

"Dear Lord, six times you've been so gracious to us. Shouldn't the seventh time, the perfect number, be with our own congregation, the ones we love the most?"

Then we prayed some more: "O Father, Jacob served fourteen years for Rachel. This is our fourteenth year of labor at Lake Avenue Church. Why shouldn't this be reward year?" Then we tried a new tack: "Lord, this is Lake Avenue's seventy-seventh year as a church; and *you* know about sevens. . . ."

Meanwhile Ray was probing. In each of the six ministries where we'd seen God meet His people in an unusual way there seemed to be only one common ingredient: time. There would be different ages, different circumstances—sometimes the people knew each other well, sometimes not at all. But they'd all had time: time to wait before God, time to linger with one another in His presence.

Ray decided that our church service format programmed out any unusual working of God. On television, every problem had to be solved in 29 or 58 minutes. In church, we were open for all God would do for us in an hour and ten minutes, but after *that*—

In January Ray called for a Week of Waiting on God. There would be nothing happening: no boards, no committees, no midweek prayer meeting, no Sunday School class affairs. . . . Many people, bless 'em, even postponed social engagements.

We would just meet to wait on God. There would be no program, nothing planned, we would just gather and *wait*. On Monday night we would wait on Him as families in our homes. Beginning Tuesday night, we would meet at church. . . .

Seven-thirty Tuesday was Heart-in-Throat Time. Would anybody come? The downstairs began to fill. The balconies began to fill. Soon the sanctuary was practically full. "You announce some big-name speaker and you hope for a crowd. You just tell 'em God's going to be here, and wow—"

Each evening some of us met for an hour or more ahead of time to pray and to throw ideas into the hopper.

"Let's study the Seventy-third Psalm in groups of twos and threes for a while. . . ."

"Let's sit quietly and let anyone lead out in singing and we'll join in. . . ."

"Let's walk out in silence tonight. . . ."

Each evening Ray and other brothers went into the sanctuary armed with maybe a dozen ideas, to use all or none. But they sat back and, mostly, the spirit of the people just pushed things along. Unless a change of pace seemed called for, people most often just lined up at the mike to share Christ. This was nothing new. But the spirit of brokenness and openness and confession was new. There were tears, there was laughter. It was something else.

We learned that waiting on God involves waiting for one another. We learned patience for the Body. We learned to honor the "lesser" members, whose right to participate probably exceeded, if anything, the others. Love in practical form!

Those with the hour-and-ten-minute clock inside them slipped away, but hundreds tasted the sweet fruits of what God does for those who *wait on Him*.

Wednesday night Ray told us about alabaster vases. (He talked very little all week.) A lot of us turned a corner that night. One woman discovered a broken vase on her floor at home, and kept it there untouched for the rest of the week, as a symbol of her own spirit.

Perhaps the high point was Friday evening for a couple of hours around midnight. One of the teenagers said, "You know, I've dreamed of the time when I'd see the entire congregation on their knees in prayer—just filling the whole sanctuary."

Nobody could have planned it. We all went to our knees. For perhaps two hours the air was full of praise. Sometimes people prayed, adoring Him. Sometimes spontaneously we sang to Him.

———————

From the little tastes of revival we've seen, when God and His people connected in very special ways, Ray and I have noticed several things:

No two situations are ever alike. God doesn't run out of ideas, but it's true that God's presence is such a cleansing fire, confession and repentance are always there. We have come to the conclusion that the Holy Spirit is a Gentleman. We have never seen excesses in behavior. He is *seemly*! But we've seen His characteristics exhibited in living color: great tenderness, great compassion for those embarrassed by their own sin, lots of tears but also lots of fun.

———————

In my Bible I have the date January 26 of that

year marked beside Isaiah 25:9:

"This is our God,. . . for whom we waited. Now at last he is here!" (*TLB*).

9

LEADERS MUST OFTEN FOLLOW FOLLOWERS

How else can Christ bring His Body together in humility?

Several years ago we were kneeling on cushions around a long, low dining table in a private hotel suite in Japan. The air was seasoned with celery and leeks and unknown things.

Through a missionary interpreter, an important Japanese industrialist was addressing Ray:

"I have come to this city and invited you to join our family at dinner so that I might ask you a question. During the past year my son has become a Christian. I admit that he was rebellious and hard to handle, and now he is a respectful, good boy. But as you know, Christians in Japan are a very small minority and are looked down upon as being low-class, disloyal both to family and to country.

"There are so many sons in Japan. Why would this have to happen to *my* son—to *me*?"

God suddenly gave the translating missionary a tender parable.

"Suppose," he said, "a shepherd wanted to take his flock to better pastures. But the way was across a raging stream, and one ram was particularly frightened and refused to budge. How would he get that dear sheep to make the trip? Why, he would take his lamb, his precious lamb, and put it on the other side first."

We watched the father's lined face as understanding dawned. A tear ran down his cheek. "Ah, so," he said.

There's almost always some trailblazer out in front of the supposed "leader." The children are ahead of their parents. Some praying person in the church is ahead of the pastor. The young people are ahead of the adults.

Of course, the "big ones" can always choose to be proud and critical and defensive.

Or they can say, "Show me. Teach me what you know. I'm such a little child, but I want all of God in Jesus Christ that I can get. I want Him in knowledge and I want Him in experience. Help me. Pray for me. Disciple me, until I get to where you are."

Oh, how hard, how rare, how sweet!

———————

It's a funny thing. A congregation of people doesn't become broken because the minister tells them to.

They get broken when *he* gets broken.

Part Two
NOW LET'S GO THROUGH A WORSHIP SERVICE

10
WHAT A WORSHIP SERVICE IS

And what it isn't

Let's start with the isn'ts first.

It isn't school.

It isn't a service club.

It isn't a church picnic.

It isn't high tea.

Churches that don't worship God turn into a multitude of things. Some become Bible information centers, where people come in with empty notebooks and go home with full ones. Some churches become fellowship centers—evangelical Kiwanis Clubs ("the more we get together, the happier we'll be"). Some become splashy publicity affairs, or missionary headquarters, or soup kitchens or counseling clinics.

In the Bible the word *worship* is variously translated "to bow," "to do reverence to," "to kiss the hand of," or other expressions to indicate an acknowledgement of the presence of Somebody Great. And *God ordained worship* to strengthen our relationship with Him.

God ordained love-making too. Think about the similarities.

Here's a wife who says, "Of course I love him! I keep his house and cook his meals, don't I?" But she seldom has sexual intercourse with him, and she almost never says, "I love you! You are so precious to me!" There you have a dry, sterile marriage, missing the foundational underpinnings of a satisfying relationship.

Sex is a ritual which God ordained to bind marriage partners together, and He tells us, "Do not deprive each other" (1 Cor. 7:5).

Worship services are a ritual God ordained, too—to bind us experientially to Him! Here's a believer who says, "Of course I love the Lord! I sponsor the youth group and teach Sunday School, don't I?" But he is seldom in the worship service, and he almost never looks right into the face of God and says, "I love you, Lord! You are truly precious to me!" There you have a dry, sterile Christian experience, missing the foundational underpinnings of a satisfying relationship with God Himself. And so He tells us, "Don't forsake assembling together" (Heb. 10:25, paraphrased).

Do you mind my saying that the two acts, worship and sex, have some similarities?

Both acts must be regular.

Both must be wholehearted.

Both must be top-priority, for which other things are put aside; they're the result of solemn commitment.

We're often told these days that married partners must arrange their schedule around love-times, stay rested for them, and make sure they're often enough and satisfying. No checkbook writing or carpet-cleaning must interfere!

Just so, a Christian must arrange his schedule around the weekly worship service. No Bible classes or missionary committee meetings must interfere. Worshiping churches will make sure that every member worships—and will insist that they do for the health of the Body. The total church program must revolve around that holy hour!

When a wife gets overactive and sex is neglected, her marriage relationship will be damaged and her husband will feel it keenly. Or when a husband. . . .

When a church member gets overactive and public worship is neglected, his or her relationship with God will be damaged.

And God will feel it keenly! Jesus said to a dinner host once, "You did not give me a kiss. . . . You did not put oil on my head. . ." (Luke 7:45,46).

When we get distracted, He notices!

11
UP WITH WORSHIP!

It stretches us to a new dimension

Have you ever thought what it would be like to live in a one-dimensional world? It would be living along a straight east-west line, and you could only travel between you and your nearest neighbor, because you had no concept of north or south, to step *off* the line and go *around*. There would be no "around" in your thinking; and two-dimensional people would look at you in pity because you had to live your whole life along one dull line.

Still, two-dimensional people are limited too, aren't they? They know north and south and east and west—and maybe they think they've "arrived." They might say, "We can go west by southwest, or north by northeast, or anywhere we want!"

But they are flatlanders—unconsciously depressed by gravity and knowing only the horizontal outlook. They have no idea of "up" and "down"—and they don't even know they're missing anything.

Non-Christians, it seems to me, are one-dimensional people. They're lonely little dots, little islands of meism, of self-love, of self-preoccupation of every kind. Their challenge in life is to get farther along their one-dimensional line to more money, more power, and so on. The only way they see to do that is to knock off the line the people ahead of them who are blocking the way to their goals. Carnal Christians have the same mind-set; you can hardly tell the difference.

Lots more Christians are flatlanders, and horizontal churches are for flatlanders.

Christian flatlanders can go lots of places. They can even cross denominational lines to hold hands and pray for each other and share and sing. They talk about the Body and missions and about spiritual gifts and evangelism. And if all they know is that two-dimensional world, they may have no idea either that they're missing anything.

Oh, when Christians learn *up*—!

A worship service where there's actually *worship* breaks through the ceiling!

Up is enlarging and releasing and purifying. *Up* is beyond atmospheric dust and smog; it's vast and limitless and beautiful. It's beyond committees and pecking orders and the push-pull of imperfect communications. *Up* has thrones and rainbows and morning stars singing together. *Up* gives meaning and perspective to flatland activities. *Up* gives hope.

Up is the Big Picture.

Up is communing with God Himself!

12
WORSHIP LOOKS UP

"Up" gives a totally new perspective

Suppose a little boy looks through the knothole of a fence to see a parade.

If he sees a clown pass by, he's tickled. If he sees a lion, he's afraid. If there's a space in between, he may think the parade's over. If someone blocks his view, he may think there's no parade at all.

But suppose a man picks him *up*. He puts him on his shoulders, above the line of the fence. Then he can see a good part of the parade all at once, and he gets the idea! Indeed, if he were higher *up*, he might see the entire parade in one view.

"Now we see through a knothole," many of us. All we can see at one moment is that our checkbook is empty, or our wife is sick, and we get thoroughly discouraged.

True worship can change all that.

13
WHOM WILL YOUR CHURCH LOVE, GOD OR SELF?

It's impossible to love both

Flatlanders may think they love each other—but basically, what motivates them is what motivates the carnal, one-dimensional Christian: love of self. For a while a flatlander church may seem to thrive, but eventually everybody will be on everybody else's nerves.

Love of self is currently the most popular heresy in evangelicalism. It may even be a sign that Christ's coming is near! "[In the last days] people will be lovers of themselves," says 2 Timothy 3:2, and when He comes He will purge away chaff from Christendom as well as elsewhere.

It often isn't all that hard to discern when a church service is simply catering to and stroking and entertaining and pleasing the people in the pews. Yet God says that only *He* is to be focused on! Indeed, He even thunders, "I am the Lord; that is my name! I will not give my glory to another" (Isa. 42:8).

When laborers love themselves, or maybe when employers do, we get strikes.

When spouses love themselves, we get divorces.

When children love themselves, we get disobedience.

When citizens love themselves, we get crime.

When churches love themselves—we get typical churches, bored, ineffective, carnal, perhaps even splitting.

Oh, but there's a better way! Let's make up our minds where our love will be placed. Let's determine together in a local body to lay our crowns at His feet.

Focusing on God Himself may totally reorganize our worship service. It may even change the building committee's mind on how to shape the new sanctuary. But it's worth all our earnest prayer, fresh thinking, and seeking the face of God.

14
GOD AMONG US

Then and now

Think about it: the Ark of the Covenant for the nation Israel was the symbol of the majestic presence of God. When it rested among them it was placed in the precious center of everything. When it traveled it went in front of all. The rest of the worship symbols were all covered with badger skins (hides of sea cows, says the *NIV*); but at the front of the train, clearly distinguishable to every eye, was the precious ark—the only item draped, says Numbers 4, in heavenly blue.

It could not be touched: it symbolized God's holiness. And yet it was near, as God is near! It was special, close, first. It visibly declared the balance of the nearness and the awesomeness of God.

Can your church's worship find ways to show His holiness, His specialness, His closeness, His firstness? It's not easy to balance His attributes in our thinking.

If He's made only "great," if He's always called "God" or "Lord," the high and lifted up One—then only the professionals are "capable" of reflecting Him, and the service will be all up front, and probably cold, intellectual, austere. God will seem that way too.

But if He's always "Jesus,"—so forgiving, so available—we can get excessive doses of laughter and applause and a general atmosphere-blend of town meeting and service club luncheon.

There's no Ark of the Covenant today, but God is more than ever among us. How do we express His presence? How do we worship Him? It will take all our Spirit-breathed ingenuity—and probably lots of trial and error—to discover how.

CHRISTIANS DON'T NATURALLY WORSHIP

Only supernaturally

Naturally, when Christians come together, they meet not God but each other. They were raised in twelve years or so of the school-type atmosphere, so they're used to assembling in a school-type manner: somewhat disciplined, somewhat orderly—but horizontal and casual.

Maybe because of this, *many Christians never worship*. They spend their lives in horizontal activities: Sunday School classes, women's meetings, home Bible studies, even church services. They extend the familiar atmosphere of the schoolroom to all their Christian activities for the rest of their lives.

They learn to know *about* God.

But they never learn to *know God*. Direct contact with Him may never have been provided for or encouraged by their churches.

What if your birthday were coming up and your friends announced they were giving you a party. You eagerly anticipated it—but finally when party time actually came, they never noticed *you*. You were off in a corner, and they talked about you as if you weren't even there! Eventually you'd get the picture—that they were just using the occasion of your birthday as an excuse to get together and enjoy one another.

Do you suppose that's the way God feels every week? Many Christians seem to use church services to talk some *about* Him, but mostly as an excuse to enjoy one another.

Only supernaturally, and through great effort and concentration by the Spirit, can Christians worship God. In any church, corporate worship must be longed for, taught, prayed for, planned ahead of time, and then demonstrated all through the service by the up-fronters. From the beginning you have to make a conscious effort to drive a beachhead and then deliberately hold that ground.

A worship service should be an intense time.

It may be with thousands in a drive-in church or with two or three at a lonely mission outpost; it may be formal or informal; but *it dare not be casual.*

(One of Ray's seminary profs used to parody the "casual" thing by draping himself over a pretend pulpit, nonchalantly tossing out "The-Lord-is-in-His-holy-temple-let-all-the-earth-keep-silence-before-Him," and then pretending to spit into an imaginary spittoon.)

Believers must gather around the *Lord!* They must get right with Him after the long week, express their love to Him again, and celebrate His presence. Psalm 89:15 says, "Blessed are those who have learned to acclaim you,. . . O Lord!"

Weekly worship is the highest corporate act of the Body of Christ. It is the visible demonstration that He is "Priority One" to us, and to our church.

We must pray over it, labor over it, shape it.

We must make our building right for it, to worship as well as we can, undistracted, inspired, uplifted.

We must center all our church schedule around it. No Bible class dare have a late party the night before. No Sunday School class will have a coffee hour which might encroach on worship time. No choir will over-practice and enter too late for heart preparation. No individual will linger outside, chatting. . . .

It's the first priority of Priority One! It's the *crème de la crème.* It's when everybody in the precious family of God is gathered, ready, unaware of each other, faces upturned. . . .

When the crowds gathered under John the Baptist's ministry, Luke 3:15 says they "were *waiting expectantly.*"

That's the idea.

16

WORSHIP IS FUNDAMENTALLY AN OFFERING

It's giving more than receiving

Back in the Old Testament days it was clear to see that worship meant giving. You came to the Tabernacle or Temple with your offering in your hand, or in your arms!—lugging it, or dragging it, maybe. It might have been wheat or oil, but often it was a sheep or goat or young bull.

Worship and giving blurred and blended. In fact, God told them, "No one is to appear before me empty-handed" (Exod. 34:20).

David wrote, "At His tabernacle will I sacrifice"—and it was to be truly a *sacrifice*. No sick sheep or lame cows; his gift had to be in perfect condition—something he'd like to have kept for himself. When David was once offered a "freebie" to use as a sacrifice, he wouldn't take it (2 Sam. 24:24). The point of the sacrifice was to give up by faith in order to see God supply—and so give Him pleasure.

And this is what worship still means today. Hebrews 13:15 says, "Through Jesus, therefore, let us continually offer to God a sacrifice of praise—the fruit of lips that confess his name."

The praise is to be continuous—which sometimes means inconvenient. It will take effort to be with your local family of God Sunday by Sunday, lifting Him up in "together" commitment.

Sometimes you may be critically busy—when every minute of the day is precious—to get something done. Well, drag that lamb of two hours' time, and come to God's house.

Sometimes you may be drained of emotion. Just the same, drag that lamb of verbalized praise to church, and offer it there.

Sometimes you'll be low on finances. Get together your sacrificial gift, and drag that lamb to the Lord's house.

You say you "don't get anything out of church"? Well, *He's* supposed to, more than you! Bring to Him your consistent, sacrificial gift of worship.

Drag that lamb!

17

WHAT SHOULD BE IN YOUR HAND WHEN YOU COME TO CHURCH

This is for everybody—up-fronters too

Your worship itself is an offering—but your worship should also *be accompanied by a gift.* Says Psalm 96:8, "Bring an offering and come into his courts."

"Now about collections," wrote Paul. "You Corinthians do the same thing I told the Galatians to do." (In other words, it's a good general plan.) "Set aside a sum of money in proportion with your income on each first day of the week" (see 1 Cor. 16:12).

(You Seventh-Day Adventists and Messianic Jews may bring it on the seventh day, but it's still weekly.)

Oh, what a thrill! What a great idea! God says to lay aside a gift to Him *weekly.* He knows very well that many of us get paid less often than that. Ray's salary comes bimonthly. We divide the Lord's amount into four equal checks—which means that when five-Sunday months come along, not of our planning, they allow us the scary thrill of giving twenty-five percent more. Remember, we don't give at our convenience; we give weekly what we've decided in our heart ahead of time to give (2 Cor. 9:7).

Here's how we do it. When the paycheck arrives we write all God's checks first, put them in pre-dated envelopes, and place them on our dresser. Every time we see them we can pray over them and anticipate the thrill of giving. Sunday morning the envelope goes into my Bible, sticking out of the pages. I've trained myself to walk in the church doors saying in my heart, "Father, I come to you bringing our offering. We love you. It's our sacrifice to tell you so."

How much do you give? Don't say, "Well, never enough!" Then you're training yourself to expect to under-give. *You can give enough.* God will show you what's the right amount in proportion to your income, and you'll have the wonderful joy of obedience in giving! *It will be big,* for you. Leave the "tipping" to unbelievers, who don't understand.

But you'll always have enough for the rest of living. Always: 2 Corinthians 9:6-8.

18

WHAT SHOULD BE IN YOUR HEART WHEN YOU COME TO CHURCH

Hand and heart must both be ready

1. *Come cleansed.* It's great to know you're going to be squeaky-clean at least once a week. Remember (if you're old enough) Saturday night baths? Did you wash your hair and polish your shoes too? Weekly worship should do the same thing for your soul.

When Isaiah had a confrontation with God, he discovered right away how dirty he was (Isa. 6:5). As soon as he admitted it God cleansed him, and it was one of the bonuses of coming to God!

Especially before communion times, 1 Corinthians 11:27-32 says that we're particularly to get cleaned up, so that we won't get sick or die as a result of taking it unworthily!

It's the end of the week and Sunday is approaching. What about you is dirty? Do you need to apologize to someone? Or apologize to God about something? Or rethink before Him some aspect of your life-style that seems besmudged by the world? Get yourself prepared for the high and holy act of coming into His presence with His gathered people.

2. *Come eagerly.* Psalm 52:9 says, "Your name

is good. I will praise you in the presence of your saints."

"Eagerly" can be translated "ten minutes early."

Or, with fair accuracy it can be translated, "I've decided we're coming back from the mountains Saturday night."

Or, "If the guests don't want to join us, they can sleep in."

Or, "I'll probably survive this headache if I just go anyway."

Or, "Forget TV; I need to be accountable to the Body."

Or, "Only the Lord Himself comes ahead of our marriage, dear, but He does come first, and I'll be with you right after church."

3. *Come praying.* See the next chapter!

19

IN THE HOLY OF HOLIES

A suggested running conversation with God, as you're on your way into church

Lord, it's a gray morning, but right now put some sunshine in my heart. We're walking into church, God: Lucy, Mark, and I. Turn them on to you, Father, and do the same for me. Thank you that they're not saying anything right now so I can talk to you.

Good morning, Mrs. McGillicutty. God, she's hardly my type, but teach me to love her this morning. Do good things for her in church too.

Morning, Elmer. Lord, thanks for Elmer. Thanks for the other ushers too.

Father, where do we sit today? Put us strategically where we'll bless people around us. Thanks, Lord, for heading Lucy down front. What a good wife.

Lord, the murmuring seems louder than usual. Forgive us all. Please, figuratively, Lord, turn down my hearing aid.

Oh, it's so good to slide into this seat. I bow before you. You're here! You've been with me all along—praise you for that—but it's special to meet you here together with the Body.

What part of yourself will you show today, Lord? You're exciting. Sometimes you show us your tenderness, your "still, small voice"—sometimes you thunder. You know my need. I'm ready.

O great God of the heavens! You are matchless. "O could I speak the matchless worth. . . ." You are worthy. You are glorious. I've used those adjectives too often, Lord. Teach me some new ones. Make me inventive in praising you.

I forgot to polish Mark's shoes. What was I doing last night that I didn't polish shoes? Oops, that's what I get for peeking. Father, forgive, shut my eyes, refocus my attention. . . .

20

GOD'S PREPARATION TACTIC

He wants us poised for living

God's strategy is silence, then action; waiting or resting, then work. Have you noticed it?

When in Genesis 1 He created twenty-four hour days, He made them "the evening and the morning." First you slept, then you worked. The mind frame was not that you work and then drop into bed exhausted to recuperate. You slept first and did your work in the stance of "restedness."

Quiet, then action.

Take when the Israelites finally arrived at the border of their Promised Land. Did they just tumble into it pell-mell and start to occupy? No, they had three days of rest and quiet, to get their orders, to think, to be totally "together" and ready.

Think about the book of Acts, which means "book of action." You have twenty-seven chapters of fast-paced traveling, witnessing, establishing churches, and so on. But there are twenty-eight chapters in the book? That's right. The first chapter is dead, boulevard stop. Preceding all the action you have a chapter of quiet, of rest, of prayer, of waiting on God.

The morning of the first day of the week—that's when we rise and worship Him. What a perfect way to prepare for the week to come!

Don't think of it as "hype" time.

It's for listening, worshiping, waiting, and silence.

Every week it's the way you get poised and ready for living.

21

ANNE'S NOTES ON ONE OF RAY'S SERMONS

"How to Worship Well; Ezekiel 44:9-16"

Adoration: that yearning for God so deep that sometimes it's painful.

Easy for a Christian to work *for* God but not minister *to* Him. We can go through worship services to "get good feelings." Worship is a ministry to God Himself.

God has made us with energy, intelligence. If we don't spend them on God, we'll spend them on ourselves.

Ezekiel 44:10,11,13. Priests who had disobeyed could only minister *in the sanctuary*. Faithful sons of Zadok were allowed to minister *to the Lord* and come near to the most holy things (vv. 15,16). *We are qualified* (see Heb. 10:19-22)! Now we must do it.

Have an attitude of desire, of pressing in, ready to bless God. "One thing have I desired of the Lord." Not natural, supernatural.

Watchman Nee: "To come into the presence of God and kneel before Him for an hour demands all the strength we possess. We have to be violent to hold that ground." It takes all God will pour into us to win that battle of attending to Him with a single eye.

Stand before God (see Ezek. 44:15). Be attentive to Him. Stand at attention. Stand as a servant stands before his master. The world says, "Don't just stand there, do something." Christ says, "Don't just do something, stand there."

It's the look that saves, but it's the gaze that sanctifies, changes us. We don't serve well because we don't "stand" well. If we would "stand" long enough, we would serve long enough.

Good things are not necessarily God's things. When we stand before the Lord He will give us all we possibly need to do—but not more than that.

Keep His charge. Hear His orders so that we can do them.

Let your future be built after you have stood before God. The secret of success: standing in the presence of the Lord.

When we come to worship we must meet God's needs first; then our own needs will be met!

Spurgeon, age 22: "While the subject of God humbles the mind, it also expands it. He who often thinks of God will have a larger mind than the man who simply plods around on this narrow globe. . . . The most excellent study for expanding the soul is the science of Christ and Him crucified, and the knowledge of the Godhead in the glorious Trinity. Nothing will so enlarge the intellect, nothing so magnify the whole of man."

Tozer: "God meant for a new convert to become a worshiper first. After that he can become a worker."

22

WHO'S RESPONSIBLE FOR THIS THING, ANYWAY?

Somebody has to make the first move

How many people have to get hungry for their church service to become a Happening before it happens?

Well, I've heard the same story you have about Dwight L. Moody—how he wasn't much until two old ladies in his congregation cried to God for him. They became the lever behind the scenes that moved the up-front person to move the people to God.

If you're a lay person reading this and you're burdened for your church, get together with a sympathetic heart and pray and pray. But watch it! Pray in sympathy and tenderness and great love; pray with an uncritical spirit; and pray that you'll be the first one changed! Then add to your prayers a life of faithful service, regular attendance, support, and optimism that God is at work answering your prayers. No bitterness, just agony and ecstasy!

And who are the up-front people who have to get concerned? This is only my own personal thinking; try it on for size:

Do you lead "two or three gathered together"?

Or teach a Bible class, a Sunday School class? Then you're up-front. You're the "pastor." No shifting of the weight to anybody else.

Or is yours a small church/group with two up-fronters, a pastor/teacher and a pianist, maybe organist? Then it will take both of you.

Suppose you're a medium-to-large church with pastor, minister of music, and organist. Then all three are your irreducible minimum.

Maybe you're First Church Downtown. You have several ministers regularly leading the worship service, plus minister of music, organist, and four paid soloists.

Then—like the sons of Kohath, all of you as a team are to bear the weight of the holy things of the Tabernacle. When the Israelites moved forward in the wilderness, there were plenty to oversee the carts and the beasts; but the Kohathites' lot was to bear the most sacred things personally on their shoulders (Num. 4:1-15).

And what does that tell you about up-front people? Well, you wouldn't call a spiritually weak person to be your pastor just because of his speaking gifts. Then neither would you call a spiritually weak person to be your church musician. No, no! Secular performances go down the street in the concert hall.

It takes all of these hearts, beating together, to make the service take wings and soar. Not because of great talent, maybe *in spite of* great talent. But just because it takes God's power to put people's hearts together—and that's the same power that raises a church service from the dead.

And when you get together, what's to be your common goal?

It won't be to follow an order of service with a

minimum number of goofs—to become a Smoothly Synchronized Team of Performers.

> (Presenting, for Your Pleasure
> on Sunday Mornings
> the Incomparable
> Rudolpho, Irena, and Dorothea.)

Your common goal—along with choir, ushers, whomever—is nothing less than to connect the people with God Himself.

Holy.

Thrilling.

Cleansing.

Warming!

Possible.

Veni, Spirite Sancte. Oh, yes, God, do come, *please.*

Come to think of it, why settle for less? Isn't that what church is supposed to be all about?

But looking around the scene, maybe that's not such a common goal. It seems to be rather *uncom-mon.* *

---

*If the up-front people aim at nothing, they can be sure they'll hit it every time.

23
THE BUCK STOPS HERE

With the up-fronters

Is it fair, is it scriptural, to put the burden of responsibility for the church squarely on its leadership? What about the ministry of the Body? What about the priesthood of all believers?

Well, without getting into the old chicken-and-egg question, I notice that when Christ sent messages to the seven churches in the book of Revelation, He sent them through the pastors (the "angels," the messengers of the Word). He considered them very key.

I know what it is, occasionally on vacation, to attend a church where the pastor has no charisma, where you just have hymns-announcements-offering-message, and nothing comes off through it all.

"What *is* the matter, Ray?" I whispered once into his ear.

"He has no theology of worship," Ray whispered back.

"Theology of worship!" Oh, right. There was no High and Holy One who was being pointed to and adored and confessed to and bowed down before.

The singing droned, "I was sinking deep in sin. . ." We were certainly sunk deep in *something*.

Yes, it's fair to put the burden on the up-fronters.

They've got to care.

They've got to cry.

They've got to bang on the gates of heaven.

They've got to pound the Throne.

They've got to accept on their backs the Burden of the Lord.

24

THOSE BEAUTIFUL WORDS, "BUT THE LORD . . . !"

There can be glory in the pew

Maybe chapter 23 discouraged you. You sit every Sunday through one of those nothing-comes-off church services.

Dear friend! At this point you need to remember those great old words of George Fox: "It is a wonderful discovery to find that you are a temple, that you have a church inside of you, where God is. In hushed silence, attend to Him. The Lord is in His holy temple."

You're sitting in church: before the service, confusion or silent sterility; during the service, well-meaning but corny slapstick. Or coldness, polished to a high glaze. Or just gray, dreary sameness. Or whatever your particular church problem is.

Do you feel that your church situation is a problem? Any time in life when you have a problem, put the problem up beside God. Then compare and see who's bigger. The book of Jonah starts out in a mess, when a man of God wasn't behaving right. Then verse 4 says, "THEN THE LORD"! GOD WAS BIGGER! And God was moving.

So you don't care for the worship in your church? Well, it isn't the "worship" you're to wor-

ship; it isn't the minister or the music—it's God.
Is He in your heart? Then apart from anything
that's happening up front, out back, around you,
anywhere—you can have your own private breakthrough into glory!

Oh, my friend, He waits to be all in all to you.
He is sufficient. You and He in a worship service
together? That's enough.

Think of all the places in the world where
Christians can't meet in His name at all. Be humble, be grateful, be sweetened in your soul. A critical spirit won't bring the glory.

Does that mean be tolerant, be satisfied with
the present state of things? No, no! Behind the
scenes, agonize in prayer for that beloved church
of yours. Find another heart that beats with yours
with revival (and who knows how to love and not
criticize) and the two of you pray and don't quit.

But in church? Don't wait for "someday," and
miss Him. You're there, He's there! Hooray! Three
cheers for God! Sing! Pray! Celebrate! Let your face
reflect the Presence!

*Your personal worship doesn't depend on
anybody else's behavior.*

25

MEANWHILE, BACK BEHIND THE SCENES

The up-fronters have to start putting it together

An organ prelude obviously doesn't fall together on a Sunday morning. It's been chosen and worked over quite a while before.

Neither does a meaningful pastoral prayer fall together on a Sunday morning. If the minister hasn't thought it all through ahead of time, pretty soon he'll be praying the same things over and over, using the same clichés. . . .

What I'm working up to is that a worship service doesn't fall together on the spot either. Unless it's been prayed through, discussed, and thought out in advance, before long it will be dull and repetitious.

First, what about for the whole year? If you're a liturgical church, you're probably observing "the Second Sunday of Advent," "the Third Sunday of Lent," et cetera. But if you're not—

Listen, *Sundays aren't cookies*. They're not to be all stamped out alike by the same cookie cutter. That means that the people responsible for shaping the services need to spread out a big annual calendar and make some decisions.

God spread out His big calendar in Leviticus 23 and He said, "Now, here you've got a special week to remember Passover. . . . And over here for a whole day the people are to deny themselves and mourn over their sins. . . . And in the middle of the seventh month, here, they're to take a whole week for fun, camping out and rejoicing with fruits and palm fronds. . . ." It was all spelled out, and it gave the year a variety of moods and activities.

When, this coming year, will your people mourn over their sins together? When will they celebrate and eat together? When will the moods of the church be extra quiet, extra noisy, extra big and important, more than usually liturgical, more than usually free? When will church have visual props or extra music or extra prayer? When will there be special efforts for community outreach? When for missions? When might you honor the young people, old people, singles, choirs, longest married? When will you laugh?

Stretch, stretch! Plan for your year of services to reach depths and heights. And all before the Lord.

26

THE PRINTED BULLETIN
A guide to a great adventure

We're such creatures of habit, aren't we!

Do something three weeks in a row, and you can place a "Do not disturb" sign on it. It's become a Sacred Tradition.

And that's how church services become dull, monotonous, repetitive.

Do you know about the father whose little son had always been in junior church and was about to graduate to the worship services, so during the week his daddy took him to visit the big sanctuary and get acquainted with it?

"Here's the pulpit where the pastor preaches to us," he said. "And here are all the pews where the people sit. And, Freddie, here in front is our service flag, where we show a star for each person in this church who's in the service."

Freddie asked, "And what are the gold stars, Daddy?"

"Well, son, the gold stars represent the men and women who have died in the service."

"Which service, Daddy," asked Freddie, "morning or evening?"

God help the poor congregation who at any given point in the service can predict with accuracy what will be happening ten minutes later!

Now, the order of worship in the bulletin will deal a death blow to the service if its purpose is just to make all those accurate predictions.

An order of worship isn't to program the up-front people—("At this time the senior minister will pray; now the assistant minister will announce the offering," et cetera)—which they read and dutifully obey while everybody watches.

Actually, relatively few are involved up front, and they can have their own notes on who's going to do what.

An order of service should program the hearts of the congregation! "Now we're going to be sorry for our sins. . . Now we will sing hymn number 121, and then we will confess to God our faults. . . ."

This gives a new concept as to who is under pressure to read the order of worship and obey— both the up-front people *and* the congregation— while *God* watches.

And let your order of worship give more "heart" than details. If you print "choral response," then the choir is locked into it and everybody knows it. Let the choir be prepared—but maybe when the time comes, God wants the people to respond in some way—to recite the Lord's prayer, to pray in silence, to sing "Spirit of the Living God. . . ." If you print "Response of Commitment" or something, you're freer—and the people are more apt to be on their toes in alertness and expectation.

Sometimes give the people little surprises. Let them not know who's going to take what. (The up-fronters know perfectly; they thought it all out in the pre-service huddle—but those are *their* secrets.) And tuck in small extras that aren't printed at all. (After you've prayed for new missionaries just going out, a soloist sings as a response "So Send I You." After you've prayed particularly for our country, the choir sings softly in unison the refrain of "America.")

Give the people special cues, through the order of worship, for behavior. How to spend the ten minutes ahead of the service. How to pray for the ushers, the first-time guests, the choir. Tuck in a poem, a quotation, a Scripture verse to stimulate the flow of their thinking on the emphasis of the worship service.

Keep them moving along. Keep them *together,* through the order of worship: now we are all praising God; now we are all thinking about what we will give Him today. We're thinking of Christ particularly now as our Shepherd, or our Redeemer, or our coming Lord.

We have a theme. We're moving along, going somewhere. Have you all caught it? Are we all together?

27

SPONTANEITY IS NOT MORE SPIRITUAL

Practiced-in-advance worship is just as biblical

Where does the idea come from that if you're "in the Spirit" you can eliminate preparation?

I'm not unsympathetic to the philosophy behind it. If the Holy Spirit is a Wind, too quickly we get rigid and un-blowable.

But all of our ideas of worship must be rooted firmly in the Scriptures, and I find in them no high praise that was just off-the-cuff. On the contrary, it seems to have been worked over and worked over.

Psalm 34 is a great psalm of praise. Did it just flow out of David like water? Well, we discover it's an acrostic with the Hebrew alphabet built into the first letter of each line. The Spirit of God inspired it, of course, but maybe it also took David a lot of work to write it.

In fact, why shouldn't God be pleased when we work very hard to worship Him the best we can?

One of the great revivals of the Bible took place when the Israelites under Nehemiah rebuilt the wall of Jerusalem. The dedication of the wall became one of the spiritual high points of Jewish history. Was it spontaneous? Not on your life.

Nehemiah divided the people in half and

walked them in two long lines in opposite directions along the top of the wall. They gave thanks as they walked around, accompanied by trumpeters specifically named. When the two lines met at the Gate of the Guard they then proceeded together to the Temple. The singers, also named, sang loudly and clearly under the direction of Jezrahiah the choir master. You just bet they practiced!

But how lovely when worship has a spontaneous *feel*. Some of our churches haven't normally printed an order of worship in the bulletin at all, and the up-fronters appeared to "hang loose." We might sing unaccompanied, or someone might break into singing something familiar and everyone picked it up. . . . It appeared spontaneous, but frankly, it's harder work. It had lots of planning, lots of prayer, and every participant had his own carefully timed order of service.

One thing is true; the more filled up with God the people are, the less prompting is needed from up front. If a people are alive with God, they feel completely frustrated if the paid staff does it all.

Whether the service is formal or informal, essentially it's a dialogue between up-front and pew. As with any sensitive conversationalist, the people who plan the service must be aware of talk-listen, initiate-respond flow back and forth. Of course they normally carry the heavy end—but is the whole service a monologue? If so, the people could have stayed home and gone to church via television.

Blessed black churches! When the people are exclaiming, "Yes!" "That's right!" "Amen!" at the end of every sentence in the sermon, they sure can't be going to sleep or mentally preparing the Sunday dinner.

The general rule, up-fronters, is to prepare and

prepare and prepare. Think where your people are, how you can lift them to God. Plan and pray through the service to the last eyelash, with each participant ready and clued in to each other.

But then if God wants to take over and make any changes, that's up to Him.

28

MAKE YOUR WORSHIP SERVICE LIKE A GAME OF PING-PONG

If at any time a worshiper drops the ball, for him the game is over

Let God initiate the process, as in Isaiah 6:1.

Let the worshipers respond, as in Isaiah 6:2 and following.

1. (Isa. 6:1)
God reveals Himself (with an opening verse of Scripture, printed, said, or sung? musical prelude? other?)

2. (Isa. 6:2-4)
Worshipers acknowledge Him with reverence and praise (call to worship? choir? opening hymn or reading?)

3. (Isa. 6:3-5)
God reveals the worshipers' sinful condition (through Scripture reading? hymn?)

4. (Isa. 6:5)
Worshipers acknowledge and confess their sin (con-

5. (Isa. 6:6)
God forgives and cleanses the worshipers (perhaps incorporated with number 6 in pastoral prayer?)

7. (Isa. 6:7)
God takes those requests and releases the burdens (choir response? Scripture verse? chorus sung by worshipers?)

9. (Isa. 6:8)
God speaks to the renewed worshiper, revealing His will and purposes (Scripture lesson? sermon?)

11. *God is pleased and seals the worshipers' decisions by His Spirit* (benediction? choir response?)

gregational prayer? silent prayer? hymn?)

6. (Isa. 6:7)
Worshipers now free to release other burdens to Him through prayers of petition and intercession

8. *Worshipers respond with gratitude and praise* (perhaps congregational hymn? sharing time? offering?)

10. (Isa. 6:8)
Worshipers respond by submitting themselves to God's will, offering themselves for whatever God desires (hymn? representative solo or anthem? altar call? other?)

12. *Worshipers are now restored, refreshed, commissioned, and they leave this encounter with God rejoicing and celebrating* (postlude?)

29

THE PRE-HUDDLE HUDDLE

Pray freshness and life into your service

Now if this precious bracket of Sunday time is really going to become something, the preaching minister, the minister of music, the organist, and all other key people are going to have to huddle before the play.

Say on Tuesday, after the pastor's day off. What's he preaching about next Sunday? (He told the minister of music last month, so the choir's been practicing the right anthem.) What's going to be the point of the whole service? How do you put together the parts to get across the point? What hymns, what organ music? Hey, what about so-and-so Scripture inserted to underline the thought? Good. A related solo number pops into your heads: could someone sing it right after the Scripture?

How can you involve the people to participate? (Their reading printed prayers or liturgies might be okay twice a year, but we're not trying to make robots.)*

How can you begin the service fresh? The pastor has been reading a call to worship lately. Instead, maybe the choir should sing Paul Sjolund's thundering "O Most High, Almighty God," with full organ. Or maybe all the people should sing unaccompanied, "Turn Your Eyes Upon Jesus."

You've been singing the Doxology to "Old Hundredth" tune for an old hundredth. Why don't you sing it to "Lasst Uns Erfreuen"? (That's "All Creatures of Our God and King.")

How can you end in a fresh way? Maybe, following the benediction, have everyone sing full voice the last phrase of Mallotte's "The Lord's Prayer": "For Thine is the kingdom and the power and the glory forever, amen!"

Every Tuesday, a huddle of up-fronters prays and rethinks.

Watch it! Don't make them dizzy with too many innovations all at once. But God knows, most of us have long been dull from too few.

---

*Maybe I'm wrong. Dr. Paul Rees told Ray and me that he heard a Church of England rector insist that God loves to be read to!

30

THE SUNDAY MORNING HUDDLE

Unity in the Spirit begins with the up-fronters

Sunday School starts at 9:30, right? Or your early worship service does, perhaps.

Eight-thirty, then, should be about right for the final huddle. You're saying you went through it all last Tuesday, and the bulletin's printed, so everything's in cement?

But that's only cold paper, and now it's got to get into the hearts of everybody who's going to help it happen.

It's time for the priests to kindle the fire on the altar! It's time to pray it in, work it up! Besides, maybe God's Spirit has some last-minute change or insertion which will lift, or delightfully surprise, or add meaning.

So the minister calls the up-fronters together into his study who are involved in the service on this particular morning. This time, for instance, it might be:

1. Harry, the minister of music
2. Gordon, the organist
3. Grace, who's going to sing a solo
4. the Pastor Emeritus who's been asked to give the morning prayer and
5. Leo, a layman, who's reading the Bible lesson.

The pastor moderates and gives a run-through of the service, item by item with the thinking behind it. He encourages the team of the morning to make suggestions.

Harry says it would stress the meaning of the anthem's words to introduce it with one verse of Scripture. Is the team in consensus? So be it.

Gordon suggests maybe the solo should be shifted to follow the pastor's sermon. (It gives a sense of beautiful flexibility to depart from the printed bulletin occasionally, when you see a better way.) But the closing hymn wraps it up better so that idea is tactfully shelved.

The timing is checked—got to keep the announcements bare-bones.

Then maybe 15 minutes for prayer. Each part of the service is prayed for: *Lord, just wrap them up in this morning's theme of your forgiving love. . . . Father, cause the reading of Psalm 32:1-6 to come alive. . . .*

Each participant is prayed for: *God bless our pastor as he preaches. . . . Fill each usher with a spirit of helpfulness. . . . Quickly "settle in" the latecomers. . . . If it's your will, don't let a baby cry! . . . Keep us from mistakes, so the concentration can be on you. . . .*

Now you're ready. (It's been a great education for Leo, and through the months many other lay people will be exposed to the philosophy of the whole service.)

But then there's Grace. She's a doll and she can really sing, but actually, she's never given any indication of spiritual life.

Suddenly, the huddle will have taught you that you can't be a mixed priesthood. You can't put strange fire on the altar! From now on, the morn-

ing team will have to be solidly united in Jesus.
Then the service will start to be together.

31

AND NOW, A WORD TO THE USHERS

There are nine verses in Scripture just for you

How important you are! If you're impeccably groomed, smell sweet, do your job pleasantly but modestly, and are spiritually sensitive—oh, what a difference to the whole service!

Of course you're prompt to begin your duties. Of course you encourage your fellow ushers with a smile and a handshake. Of course you smile at all comers and seat them courteously. Of course you usher almost in silence. A big grin and a whisper! That's you. They can read your lips.

But beyond those things, have you thought of these fine points? The farther forward you are in the sanctuary, the more you must keep your body movements to a minimum. During prayers, Scripture readings, musical numbers, or speaking, stand still. Check discreetly with your eyes for vacant seats, but don't move; you'll distract. And of course—politely, gently, don't let anyone else move!

Wonderful if your head usher encourages you to seat latecomers at certain times and also only in certain places—in the back or in the balcony—so they won't break attention.

And then that beautiful section from James 2:1-9, the ushers' portion, is just for you. It says to never fawn. Never discriminate. No play-ups, no put-downs.

Think of it: Philippians 2:7 says that for our sakes Jesus "made himself nothing." The Greek word is *kenosis:* He divested Himself; He took off his royal robe. When He came from heaven to earth, as Lightfoot says, "He stripped Himself of the insignia of majesty."

And that, ushers, is the way all those dear people are before Him. Their clothing means nothing. Don't see pearls or furs. Don't see patches or holes. He doesn't. See precious people—in Christ, or needing Him. *"Accept one another,"* says Romans 15:7. Or as *The Living Bible* puts it, "Warmly welcome each other into the church, just as Christ has warmly welcomed you."

32

THE BURDEN OF THE ORGANIST

Waiting for the sermon to make it happen is too late

How do people connect with God?

No doubt about it, it's mystery and miracle.

I guess we all realize that in the majority of churches most people only get connected to people.

No wonder most congregations are judgmental! "God's way off in heaven, but *George* is in the pulpit, and that George—ugh! . . ."

And then there's you, the organist. If your church is a people-with-people situation, then you're there for them to *review*. You're too loud, too soft, too fast, too slow, too fancy, too plain or you're just not quite on this morning.

But if you can bring them to God! *IF!*

Here, like Job, I want to put my hand over my mouth. Who am I even to offer suggestions?

Well, I confess personally much failure and a little success; but the little success I've known has been so tremendous it's worth scratching and clawing for!

My organist friend, whether you're superbly trained or barely adequate, you can bring them to God, IF—

1. IF you're with Him first yourself. If you're in

fellowship with Him because you've been personally cleansed by that New Testament Lamb, Jesus Christ.

2. And IF you're in fellowship with the others, too, united in heart in your common spiritual redemption, and united in heart because, as in a good marriage, you're guarding your fellowship and working at it. (You say you don't think the other up-fronters have experienced Christ's salvation? Are you sure this is the right organ job for you?)

3. And IF the *Word of God* is in your music—yes it can be there—so that your keyboards communicate His specific message.

You have it in 2 Chronicles 5:11-14:

1. Verse 11 says the priests had undergone their own personal purification rites. (Man, this means *weekly!* This doesn't just mean you were saved twenty-five years ago.)

2. Verse 13 says the instrumentalists were united as one with the singers and others. (Do you need to apologize to Harry before the Sunday service?)

3. Verse 13 also gives the message of their music *in words:* they praised and thanked the Lord with, "He is good; his love endures forever."

Verse 14 gives the result: the glory of the Lord came into the Temple in brightness and power.

Still, any one-two-three formula is too pat. Enlist anybody and everybody to pray for you. Don't be too proud to ask! Will some faithful prayer warriors pray in the deacons' room straight through the service as it happens? Will two in the congregation be praying for you every time you play? Will you seek to purify your own life continually so that your whole personality communicates God to them?

God isn't really being coy and playing hard to get. He wants to come among His people in reality and renewing.

A young woman in a former congregation of ours had just lost her job and she came into the sanctuary completely bewildered and discouraged.

That morning the organist happened to be playing "Be Still, My Soul," *Finlandia* tune:

The Lord is on thy side!
Bear patiently the cross of grief or pain;
Leave to thy God to order and provide—
In every change He faithful will remain.

As on the Damascus road, God in that moment confronted her in the way. She told the congregation later that those words, like the brightness of the noonday sun, made her fall on her face and say, "What shall I do, Lord?"

It was the moment of a new start in her life.

33

THE PRELUDE

It isn't supposed to come off like restaurant dinner music

You're the organist at First Church and it's prelude time. You slide onto the bench. The voices are already raucous and rising. Two portly men are standing in the front of the sanctuary, before everybody, guffawing over something together. A junior high boy pounds down the side aisle.

O God, we're going to connect these people with you? You're kidding! This is the opener of a high school basketball game. It's got everything but popcorn and peanuts.

And then there are my critical insides. (Mrs. McGillicutty is now standing up to wave to the ladies she saved seats for.) *Lord, how are you going to connect my insides with you?*

A prelude isn't supposed to come off like restaurant dinner music. It's background, all right, but it's background to silence not background to noise.*

You're on your bench and you have this dream: your music is going to hush them, lead them to

---

*I admit most preludes aren't background to silence. A lady told an organist friend of mine, "Young man, your preludes are so loud, I can't hear what my friends are saying!"

silence, then to worship. You're going to start connecting them with God.

How?

1. About the volume. Years ago my first attempts to quiet the people were demonic. I'd work up to a huge climax and cut off . . . Let Mrs. McGillicutty find herself screaming in church and maybe she'd be embarrassed enough to quit.

Actually, though, variety in volume is crucial. It will cut down the talking. Work up, work down. Be suddenly soft. (Forget the suddenly loud.) Sometimes pause altogether between numbers.

2. Enlist the minister's help. He can come in before your prelude, or at a stopping place during it, and speak to the people about the need for silence, for heart preparation, about the purpose of the prelude; and he can ask them to find their seats quickly and get right to God, et cetera. Just a few sentences each Sunday—maybe sixty seconds' worth—will start paying off.

Then he can sit bowed in prayer and set an example!

3. Do you know the power of a hymn? Brother, between those two hard covers in your hands you've got dynamite. Play your classical repertoire, of course—as lofty and intricate as your skill allows, but for connecting people with God, HYMNS ARE WHERE THE POWER CONNECTS.

34

HYMNS ARE WHERE THE POWER CONNECTS

The "flesh" of music becomes Word—and we behold His glory!

Read 1 Corinthians 14:2-12 to see that worshipers have got to understand what's going on. Organist, if your preludes and offertories are always classical unknowns how are your people going to get the message? The apostle Paul talks about flutes and trumpets and says if they don't play a clear melody, where's the communication?

Let's focus in, now.

How do you communicate? *How can the notes you play do anything to the hearts of your people?*

All right, so you're going to try hymns for part of the prelude time. Don't just flip the hymnbook pages and start in. No, no! TO CONNECT YOUR PEOPLE WITH GOD takes strategy—all the strategy you can scratch, claw, and dig for.

You know your people. Pick out hymns they know the words to (at least one verse). And pick hymns whose subjects make sense when you put them together. Gradually they'll get the purpose behind your playing. They'll start to THINK as they listen.

What subjects? Intensely personal ones. Out of

your playing, you want WORDS to pop into their heads:

"My God, how wonderful Thou art! . . ."

"Nearer, still nearer. . . ."

If your music is to be the background to what they're doing, you want to give powerful suggestions so they'll *do the right thing.* (Not to find out how Uncle John's gallbladder is this week, but to get quickly, individually, to the Person of God.)

"I need Thee, O I need Thee! . . ."

Get through to them—oh, get through! This breakthrough of your spiritual message into their consciousness can be the most important key to their mentally turning off each other and turning on to Christ. That's why key, familiar phrases must be strongly fervent.

(Organist to people: "I believe this with all my heart. I'm playing it this way so you'll get it and believe it too!")

Remember, you're not edifying yourself. Use what blesses *them.* Pull some hymns from the memories of the old-timers, some that are contemporary. (Easy does it; wrap it all up in tenderness and dignity.) Catch the ears of the little ones: "Praise Him, Praise Him, All Ye Little Children" will speak to the tiniest tot—and his grandfather.

Be sure to give plenty of variety in volume. What a trap we've fallen into lately, thinking "worshipful" meant "quiet"! How inhibited we've become, how insipid our church services! Can you believe it —when Nehemiah led the people in worship the joy of Jerusalem was heard in all the surrounding country (see Neh. 12:43)! Sometimes worship is loud: "Shout for joy, all ye peoples!" (God, you're so great!) Sometimes worship is quiet: "Be still, and know that I am God." (I wait before you, Lord.)

Organist friend, ring the changes! "How do I love Thee, God? Let me count the ways. . . ."

35

PLAIN OR FANCY?

There are always those musicians who feel that hymns are beneath them

A hymn is like a woman. Her intrinsic beauty and worth are absolutely established. But you can sure dress her up or down according to the occasion.

Hymns in church? Sometimes up, sometimes down.

If a choir has sung a number of anthem-type hymn arrangements lately, it's probably time to sing one right out of the hymnbook—one that touches the heart, straight and sincere. Your people will hum it the whole next week.

An organist can lift new beauty out of old hymns by using many of the stunning hymn arrangements on the market today—arrangements which still bring out the melody line so that the message is clearly there. But maybe another time he'll play, "Jesus Loves Me, This I Know" simply, genuinely, one chord at a time and no passing tones.

Organist, are you gifted in arranging? Then shelve old Bach for a while, and do exactly what he did in his day for his congregation: take your people's current favorite hymn tunes, make the melodies stand out strong and clear, and give them backgrounds as patterned as old lace.

One warning, though. Too many embellished hymns are like too many fat people in one room. You begin to long for a little bony structure to show; you begin to try to think what the original is really like underneath.

Singers and players, do you know what will make your hymns most beautiful? Live right, friends; live right.

36
SUGGESTIONS FOR NONCREATIVE ORGANISTS

And for other organists who go dry. I'm going to keep this book around; I'll be needing it.

Organist, you're preparing for Sunday's prelude.

Suppose this Sunday you want to encourage people to meditate on God's leadership. You could:

1. Start with "Lead On, O King Eternal," melody line only with a solo trumpet stop. (Catch the ear of Mrs. McGillicutty.)

2. Move on to "He Leadeth Me"; "Guide Me, O Thou Great Jehovah"; "Lead, Kindly Light"; "Where He Leads Me"; "O Master, Let Me Walk with Thee." For the old-timers "Footprints of Jesus"; for the teenagers "I Have Decided to Follow Jesus."

Just use the ones *your* church people really know and respond to.

———

Or suppose you'd like them to meditate on the quiet of God.

1. Do they know "The Lord Is in His Holy Temple"? Do it high on one manual, no pedals. "Let all the earth keep silence before Him. . . ."

2. Then maybe "Dear Lord and Father of Mankind," with a pretty 16' stop. "Forgive our feverish ways. . . ." (The Jones family have just settled into their pew after an hour's nightmare of spilled

cornflakes and lost socks.)

3. How about "Near to the Heart of God": "There is a place of quiet rest. . . ." and use some chimes.

Or you want "praise" for your theme. What a subject! And so much to choose from.

1. No tremolo—maybe "All People That on Earth Do Dwell," Old Hundredth in its original rhythm, crisp and attention getting.

2. No pause, straight into "When Morning Gilds the Skies," light but bright! Repeat it, bigger and bigger—

3. Suddenly soft, into "Praise Him, Praise Him, All Ye Little Children." Why not?

4. Maybe "Hallelujah! What a Saviour!"—the chorus of "Our Great Saviour," Hyfrydol tune—

5. Then "O Could I Speak the Matchless Worth"—build it to a finish of fanfare and thunder.

———————————

How many subjects can you minister to them about? You'll never run out. Many subjects are obvious from your hymnal's topical index. Put together "Near to the Heart of God"; "Nearer, Still Nearer"; "Nearer, My God, to Thee"; "O for a Closer Walk."

Put together "All Hail the Power of Jesus' Name"; "The Name of Jesus"; "How Sweet the Name of Jesus Sounds"; the chorus of "He Keeps Me Singing"; "Take the Name of Jesus with You."

Put together "Holy Bible, Book Divine"; "Thy Word Is Like a Garden, Lord"; "Break Thou the Bread of Life"; "Open My Eyes, That I May See"; "More About Jesus."

Put together "Holy Ghost, with Light Divine"; "Breathe on Me, Breath of God"; "Spirit of God, Descend upon My Heart"; "Fill Me Now."

Don't put *any* of them together unless they're meaningful to *your* congregation. Use what turns them on.

If you're gifted at arranging, transposing, modulating—my friend, be challenged to the hilt. Put them together like a sermon, with valleys, plains, and peaks in perfect proportion; with the right "feel" as you change keys to increase the fervor or to subside. And all of it to put across the message in the most vivid way possible.

And if you can't do these things? If it's in your heart, you can still pack a wallop through hymns.

Plan your theme.

Pick out your hymns.

Arrange them in order of message, key changes, dynamics, emotion, et cetera.

Practice like crazy.

Next Sunday morning you'll be ready to prop open your pages and *tell 'em the story.*

37

WHAT HYMNS? ALL CHURCH STAFFERS, TAKE NOTE

"After all, I've had *years* of training, and only the best is good enough for God," signed, the Flesh.

A Communion cup is a Communion cup is a Communion cup. It is set apart from all common uses to a sacred use. Never mind if it's cleverly shaped or if the silver's wearing thin. Its use is settled; its contents bring blessing.

Whichever one you are, O Communion cup, you are beautiful because you are in Jesus' hands to be used.

———

A Christian is a Christian is a Christian. He is potentially perfect and full of glory; he is in heaven's eyes complete; he is beautiful. He may have warts and moles, be halt, maimed, or blind; he may be shaped like a pear or wrinkled like a prune.

O believer—whoever you are, God's heart is full of love for you and I want my heart stretched until it's full of love for you too.

———

A tried-and-true hymn is a tried-and-true hymn is a tried-and-true hymn. It is no longer on trial; only my judgment of it is. It may be trite, it may be emotional, it may be (horrors!) subjective instead of objective.

O lowliest, poorest little hymn, I bow my head

and acknowledge that you probably have brought more blessing to the church than I personally ever will. Forgive my judgmental spirit. I may not use you, but I will rejoice when others do. The members of the Body are varied but all precious; their hymns are varied but all precious too. Forgive my student-day snickers. I've put away childish things.

––––––––––

The theme of the morning's service is God's love. The opening hymn is "Love Divine, All Love Excelling"; the minister is going to read the last soaring verses of the eighth chapter of Romans; why shouldn't the organist play for the offertory "Jesus Loves Even Me"?

––––––––––

The choir anthem this Sunday is contemporary and dissonant and loud! It's great—exciting—but a few white-haired saints may experience a little future shock. God bless them, they won't be around forever to be ministered to. Pastor, let them read or recite the Twenty-third Psalm. Organist, play for them "Tell Me the Story of Jesus," or "In the Sweet By and By," or "Rock of Ages."

This isn't politicking. It's being sensitive to all the flock and bringing a balanced diet to the service.

It may even keep Mrs. McGillicutty from changing her membership over to the Church of the Good Shepherd.

38
INSTEAD OF A PRELUDE

There are lots of ways to prepare for worship

Did you ever have your congregation enter in total silence? We did once. We had the ushers whisper the word. It was fantastic. People really prayed. Or read their Bibles. Or at least their bulletins. No doubt a few didn't get the word and thought the organist was sick, or the organ had blown a fuse.

Do you have a singing congregation? Go from favorite hymn to favorite hymn, playing just enough introduction for the people to identify it, and let them sing along—seated—on first verses only. No hymnbooks. The minister of music or any singing man can be seated up front to start them out.

Other instruments are a wonderful change. A violin, a flute, a cello, a harp—

A guitar? Well, you know your church, I don't.

39

BODY LANGUAGE IS POWERFUL COMMUNICATION

When you're in church, how do you look?

Worshipers all have to be taught how to worship. We may have gone to church for years and yet never developed our worshiping muscles!

Let none of us assume we know how. In fact, scenes of heaven in the book of Revelation seem so foreign to us we probably know much less than we think we know.

But let's deal with the obvious.

Churchgoer, *when* do you walk in the door? Henrietta Mears used to say, "If you're not ten minutes early, you're late!"

The idea is to express eagerness. If you stand around yakking outside, you give off the aroma that you consider meeting people more important than meeting God. If you rush up in your car at the last minute, you give the impression that you consider bed more important.

How do you walk in the door? Come in meekly from the back entrance. (From the front you distract.) Tiptoe in, *sneak* in. Assume that of course everyone seated is already seeking to connect with God. Greet the usher with a smile and a whisper.

Now, using as little motion as possible, go all the way to the front row if you're first—or fill in immediately behind. That way your body is going to set the pattern for worshipful behavior behind you and you won't be disturbed by those who come after you.

Body language! Oh, what it does for the Body! Slide into your seat, shut out those around you, and bow very low in obvious, earnest prayer. Talk about it all to God and don't hurry. Confess your sins, get clean and ready. When you've really lingered before Him then get into the Book. Not the pew Bible but your own; read, mark, pray, think, be quiet. Gorgeous!

Body language! Do you understand it? If you really understood that you were in face-to-face encounter with Jesus Christ, could you slouch back in your seat with right foot over left knee? Could you keep your head up, swiveling to look around? God help us all!

Body language! Every physical body sets the mood for the twenty or thirty people situated around and behind him. Earnestness must show! When you pray, *pray.* (When Hannah moved her lips, the spiritual life of her day was at such a low ebb, Eli her priest thought she was drunk. He didn't even recognize earnest praying when he saw it!) When you listen, *listen.* A guy can turn his head to gaze admiringly at his girl and wash worship down the drain for twenty people sitting behind him. Or he can turn his head to nod at his girl a confirmation of a point in the sermon, and behind him twenty hearts will beat faster.

Bodies talk volumes.

40
THE BODY OF CHRIST NOURISHES ITSELF IN WORSHIP

Every member feeds every other member

What do you suppose are, say, the three most important contributions you make to God and to each other when you gather with other believers to worship? I'm thinking about it, and I can suggest three: total, earnest concentration; sincerity; and prayer.

Total, earnest concentration. Even a mother with wiggly kids can learn, with her eyes fixed up front and heaven on her face, to pinch! Pinching is the perfect discipline for church. As she becomes expert she can keep her hands positioned so that even the most alert person behind her could not possibly detect it. And she can learn the precise pressure of a pinch which will send the message without producing an overreaction.

Sincerity. Think about it. You're all singing: "See, from His head, His hands, His feet, Sorrow and love flow mingled down. . ." In the middle of the phrase some singer grins hello at a friend, and something's lost that cannot be regained.

Prayer. Christians united in worship must be taught when concentration of prayer is particularly needed. Recognize the red-flag signals: a baby begins to cry, a fire engine clangs by outside, somebody gets sick. Especially when the preacher is coming to the clincher of his sermon with an important appeal for response from the listeners—from somewhere, raucous kids are released from Sunday School.

The magnetic field of the Holy Spirit often becomes a field of battle. Learn to smell war in the air, and bear down in prayer.

———————

Every congregation has a choice to be one of two things. You can choose to be a bag of marbles, single units that don't affect each other except in collision. On Sunday morning you can choose to go to church or to sleep in: who really cares whether there are 192 or 193 marbles in a bag?

Or you can choose to be a bag of grapes. The juices begin to mingle, and there is no way to extricate yourselves if you tried. Each is part of all. Part of the fragrance. Part of the "stuff."

41

UP-FRONTERS, YOUR BODIES MATTER TOO

Unless you're buried behind an altar rail or in a console pit

Interesting that most up-fronters are not only audible but also visible. Are you going to ask God to make eternity come ringing through your words and music—and then do it with wooden faces and stiff backs?

No, no.

Now, this is delicate. The difference between the externally flamboyant and theatrical and the wholly enthusiastic body, soul, and spirit, may be a difference that is discernible only because of your life all week long; because of your asking God to make you come across in sincerity; and because of the whole atmosphere of a prayer-backed service.

When Ray was in preaching class at Princeton, his prof wouldn't let the students preach standing back on their heels. In that stance they didn't care much about what they were saying. They had to preach leaning forward, standing on the balls of their feet. Body language! *I care. I love you. I believe this. Dear flock, listen.*

Organist, when you play, sing. For one thing, your own singing and breathing will be a check on the tempo. But more, you're together, you're part of them. *This is not just an organ job to me. I'm praising too; I'm asking Him too; I'm doing what you're doing; I'm with you in this, dear people.*

Organist, if you must change stops during a prayer, do it quickly, then tune your heart to God. Or don't set up the registration for your next cue and then blank out. Listen to everything!

Minister of music, is there a responsive reading? You read too. And let your face be part of all the action. Rejoice with those who rejoice, and weep with those who weep. Grapes in the bag together!

All up-fronters, when the sermon time comes don't you dare walk out—not even if you have three consecutive services. (How will the people know you don't go out for coffee all three times? It hurts morale.) Give the preaching all your attention no matter how many times you've heard it. Use your Bible. Take notes. Pray for the preacher.

How God must love those of His children who are faithfully involved in preaching or playing or singing for three or four services every Sunday! What a precious, special breed they are: they with the slightly numb backsides, and serious attention on their beautiful faces.

42
HOW TO SING A
CONGREGATIONAL HYMN

In one easy lesson

---

*One preacher once stopped a hymn in the middle and cried out in desperation, "If you people don't sing, I can't preach!"

43

ORGAN BRIDGES

Don't just diddle around

The first congregational hymn is over, the amen has been sung, everybody's sitting down, and the organist is supposed to keep playing for a moment while ushers seat latecomers.

Right?

This is the great moment of truth—the great exposure of the organist's personal religion.

Did I overstate? Well, it's the great reflection of the organist's personal opinion of the worship service.

Organist, don't just diddle around.

Say something!

Has the congregation just sung "O Worship the King"? Continue full organ with "Come, Thou Almighty King," and pray He'll come.

They've just sung "O Worship the King" and now the pastor is going to pray? Well, then, back down and bridge into "King of my life, I crown Thee now; Thine shall the glory be. . . ."

Maybe the pastor would begin his prayer on the "King" theme.

Or they've just sung, "Praise Ye the Lord, the

Almighty" or "The God of Abraham Praise." Something big! How about straight into the chorus of "To God Be the Glory. . . . Praise the Lord, praise the Lord, Let the earth hear His voice!"

Romans 12 says to be fervent in spirit. That includes church organists as they play bridges after opening hymns. Don't sound like a prayer response. Get underneath it and urge it along. Play it with heart!

————————

It was the first Sunday in December in one of our former churches. Advent Season!

The opening hymn was "O Come, O Come, Emmanuel." The organ followed by bridging into the old children's chorus "Into My Heart." ("Come into my heart, Lord Jesus. . . .")

Immediately, two pastors read Psalm 24 antiphonally:

"Lift up your heads, O you gates;. . .that the King of glory may come in."

"Who is this King of glory?"

"The Lord strong and mighty, the Lord mighty in battle. Lift up your heads, O you gates;. . .that the King of glory may come in."

"Who is this King of glory?"

"The Lord Almighty—he is the King of glory."

Without a pause a tenor soloist began to sing,

"Thou didst leave Thy throne
And Thy kingly crown
When Thou camest to earth for me;
But in Bethlehem's home
Was there found no room
For Thy holy nativity:
O come to my heart, Lord Jesus!
There is room in my heart for Thee!"

The organist followed a half step higher in key
with an urgent repetition,

>"Into my heart, into my heart,
>Come into my heart, Lord Jesus. . ."

There was a real sense of prayerful expectancy
over the people for His very special presence.
And He was there.

44

ABOUT THE SPECIAL MUSIC

If any

No, there isn't any value in adding to an up-front performance just in the spirit of "the show must go on."

Minister of music, why should you arrange for "special music," anthems, solos, duets, instrumental numbers, and so on? Because the more ways in which we can get the members of the Body to "talk" to one another, the better. They need to communicate, participate, testify, praise, exhort, encourage—everything; and if the Spirit has gifted them to do it through music, that's part of the participation.

Then the music becomes *real.*

Believers communicate with believers, and the vehicle is music. (Occasionally it might be believers communicate with unbelievers, urging them to come to Christ.)

Then how will you choose the music that is special? Well, you see what's going on in that particular service: what the pastor's preaching about, if missionaries are being welcomed home, or a new Christian is giving a testimony, or it's "youth emphasis" Sunday, or whatever—and you build on that.

So the whole service will then become a piece.

Of course you'll look for variety of presentation: a big, ornate choir number; a simple, childlike hymn for the choir to sing; a duet, a flute, a mixed quartet, a violin. . . .

But first you look for *heart* in the performers. Then you choose the musical message that will fit the performers' spiritual experience as well as fit the need of the morning.

Where do these come from?

From God the Spirit.

Then how do you find "special music"?

Ask Him.

45

THE PASTORAL PRAYER

It's a demonstration of a representative form of government

When a congregation is together in worship, any prayers ought to be total-participation situations. We don't have the right to waste the saints' precious time with anything less than that which involves everybody.

This gives congregational prayer a choice of these forms, among others:

1. *Silent Prayer.* Let it be really silent! We can't concentrate on talking to Him against background music. Subjects for praying may be suggested by the minister in brief, occasional words.

2. *Audible, spontaneous prayer by all simultaneously.* Some Christian groups around the world always pray this way; most never do. It can be stimulating and refreshing.

3. *Audible prayers read in unison from a prayer book or bulletin.* Perhaps the best rule here is, if you *always* do it, consider quitting for awhile; if you *never* do it, consider doing it occasionally.

4. *Voluntary "sentence prayers" on behalf of all.* Our own church people have enjoyed this, even with a thousand people together. The rules are: speak up so all can hear, and pray only one or

two sentences. Often we've participated on a specific theme of praise or petition.

5. *Several laymen designated in advance to pray on behalf of all*. These can stand and pray in turn from their pews or they can come together at the pulpit first and take turns there. How precious this method has been for us overseas in multi-language situations, when godly laymen prayed, each in his own tongue, on behalf of various segments of the people!

6. *One pastor in the pulpit praying on behalf of all*. Variations of this are several pastors in the pulpit—or a pastor and a layman—praying conversationally back and forth on behalf of their people.

Again, it must be stressed that this is representational praying! It is on behalf of the whole Body. No pastor has the right to pray, "Lord, forgive us for communicating poorly with each other" because Deacon Charlie Jones forgot to tell him about a business item, and he hopes Charlie will get the point and get with it. Neither is it Sneaky Announcement Time: "Lord, bless the Shnooker family whose aunt died last Thursday," or "Lord, bless the Sunday School picnic coming up this Friday afternoon at five. . . . Bless all those who bring an extra dozen cookies. . . . Help them to remember it will be held in the high school gym in case of rain. . . ."

No, this prayer is *on behalf of all the family of God*, praying in their stead to Him.

We get the picture from 1 Kings 8 and 2 Chronicles 6, King Solomon's prayer on behalf of all his people.

His posture varied. He was up on a platform out of doors; sometimes he faced the Temple; sometimes he faced the people; sometimes he stood, sometimes he knelt down before them, reaching his arms toward heaven.

His subject matter was consistent: he referred 94 times to God, 81 times to the people of God. His prayer was to relate them to each other.

It was all carefully planned. It had symmetry and form: an invocation, a blessing, a time of petition, another blessing. It concerned God's glory, sin, trouble, obedience, disobedience, God's promises, God's forgiveness, the people's spiritual history. It had lofty themes, majestic scope! How lifting; how realistic, but how stretching congregation-wide prayers should be!

And what a part we people in the pew must play! If that one who prays represents *me*, I must be continually echoing an amen in my heart: "That's right, Father. . . . Yes, do it. . . . I agree to what he's saying. . . ." My listening must be in active, aggressive partnership.

Variations in posture? Wouldn't it be glorious if we were free enough of our inhibitions to stand, sit, or kneel as our individual hearts required, lifting arms or not, eyes closed to all around, but ears and hearts opened to heaven?!

As Solomon finished his prayer in 2 Chronicles 7:1, fire came out of heaven and all the people fell flat on the pavement.

Words fail me.

THE OFFERTORY

Oops,
Mrs. McGillicutty is at it again

The prelude and the offertory are the two points in many a service that signal Happy Talk Time.

They also are the two points when usually nothing's doing except the organ.

Organist, does that tell you something?*

---

*Everything that was said in chapters 32 to 38 and 48 to 52 applies here.

WHY AM I WRITING? WHY ARE YOU READING?

Let's stop a minute and check motives

All this can't be a self-improvement course. Or church-improvement course.

Father, if I'm writing this because I'm an "author," forget the whole thing. Settle me back to rest anonymously and contentedly in your love.

Lord, if these readers are reading to become "Super-Worshipers"—

(*"None of the other churches in our town know how to worship, but boy, do we. . . ."*

"All the rest of these people sitting around me in church are just aware of one another, but I'm aware of God. . . ."

"If we can just latch onto some of these exciting techniques we can lure all the saints out of the church-up-the-street and into our church. . . .")

God, we're unprofitable servants. May the hot flames of your purifying judgment sizzle and crackle within us until ego is but gray ash, wafting impotently away.

Lord, this is all for you. This is to give you pleasure. This is to make you delighted with us!

CHURCH PEOPLE, GET WITH IT!

If you sing, *sing*. If you play, *play*. If you preach, *preach*.

There is nothing so important in religion as wholeheartedness.

The psalmist said, "I will praise you, O Lord, with all my heart" (Ps. 9:1). "I will sing of the love of the Lord forever" (89:1).

If I were a betting person, I'd bet the worst malady of church people everywhere isn't poor taste or singing sour notes; it's lack of conviction.

Friends, do what you do with intensity. This doesn't necessarily mean being garish or sensational or loud. It simply means that whatever you do you communicate—audibly and visibly—to God and to one another. So do only what is meaningful; eliminate all else from worship; and then what you do, do with all your heart.

Think of the emotion built into our hymns:

"Thou, O Christ, art all I want;
More than all in Thee I find."

"O joy that seekest me through pain,
I cannot close my heart to thee."

"The dearest idol that I have known,
Whate'er that idol be,

Help me to tear it from Thy throne
And worship only Thee!"

"That soul, though all hell
Should endeavor to shake,
I'll never, no, never,
No, never forsake!"

"Jesus, Thy blood and righteousness
My beauty are, my glorious dress.
'Midst flaming worlds, in these arrayed,
With joy shall I lift up my head!"

Joy! Glory! Hallelujah! What excitement! How dare we play or sing a message such as this like weak tea and toast?

Take another example:

"Face to face with Christ, my Saviour—"

We can't sing and play it full of cream puffs and marshmallows.

Face to face—just Him and me?

My God, I'll never sing it or play it again until you teach me how to communicate it.

49

CLASSICAL ORGAN LITERATURE HAS ITS PLACE

If you keep it in its place

Praise God for all the beauty He's inspired in this world! Praise Him for the proportions of arches and columns and spires in St. Stephen's Church in Vienna! Praise Him for the colors that glow from the windows of Canterbury Cathedral in South England! Praise Him for so-called "secular" beauty, too: the architecture of Lima, the flower beds of Tivoli!

When God made us in His image, one manifestation of that is that we are busy little "creators." Look down from any airplane and marvel at it.

So praise God for every piece of good, classical music; yes, and praise God *with* it, too—IF, IF, IF! It must have a spirit about it that makes it fit. It must be very special if it's to be drafted for God's service. The world is full of secular music situations. Most secular music should stay right there.

And sacred music in your church? Well, it depends on *which piece.* Would you want any ordained minister in the world to preach in your pulpit? Then neither does all sacred music fit your church. An "Ave Maria" at First Methodist would be a little grotesque.

But more: a prelude or choir anthem that's

right for a college campus church may be all wrong for a rural community. Where are your people? Respect them, honor them, and *meet them where they are.*

"Yes," many voices will clamor, "but church music—and sermons, too—should also lift and educate." May I gently suggest that a leader has to be out in front *a little way,* but not too far. If the gap's too wide, they'll never follow him.

And anyway, sniff the aroma of that "education" comment. Was that a haughty spirit talking? Maybe the church musician or the preacher needs to learn more from their people in certain areas than the people need to learn about music or theology. Listen to your dear flock. Get to know them deeply, their needs, their joys. Then lift and educate and make them what they could never have been without your ministry.

But also—*scratch 'em where they itch.*

———————

So how do you pick what you're going to play, organist? Well, here's the point: never play a single note without meaning.

Never!

To the extent that you put in filler which is excelsior and sawdust, to that extent your people will be tempted to grow dull and ho-hum as you play.

Even a wordless classical number must create the spirit of connecting the people with God—or else forget it. Maybe you'll do it through George Bohm's "Lord Jesus Christ, Be Present Now" (meditative, pre-Bach). Maybe you'll do it through Sigfried Karg-Elert's "Lord Jesus Christ, Be Present Now" (big, ornate, twentieth century).

And, oh, there's a rich wealth of organ literature to use! Search constantly to find the treasures, those pieces through which the spiritual heart of the composer glows—pieces that will beautify and heighten the effect of the service.

But if the piece isn't doing the job, shelve it.

Be honest: are you ever tempted to show off? Walk out the door and go get a cup of coffee. Hassle it out with God and don't come back to your work until self is put down and you're ready to minister—only minister.

Only minister?

Ministering is absolutely the most!

Lord, what can we do next Sunday that will break into glory?

50
ESSENTIAL INGREDIENTS FOR A HAPPENING

We were sitting in a little theater in Disneyland, watching an old film clip of Walt Disney philosophizing on what makes a good movie. Back he leaned in his leather chair.

"Nobody could have predicted how well 'Snow White' was going to do," he said. "Not in our wildest dreams. Heady with success, we put together another, 'Alice in Wonderland.' But do you know—it never went over very well.

"So we sat back and tried to analyze why. And we came to the conclusion that 'Snow White'—and every successful production—had two ingredients: laughter and tears.

"That was a milestone discovery," said Mr. Disney, in his modest, chatty way. "After that, everything we turned out had to have both laughter and tears."

Ray and I grabbed that one. Every conference we speak at must have laughter and tears. Every speaking date, every worship service. At least we can aim for it, have it in mind, ask God for it. A happening—a real, to-be-remembered occasion—needs truth (doctrine—thoughtful, nitty-gritty substance), but it also needs to be clothed in laughter and tears.

———————

In the deep jungles of Peru, Ray and I were with Wycliffe missionaries when God met them in a fresh way. Some of those strong men wept so hard before their brothers, they were literally supported by friends who came and stood with them as they spoke. And yet God the Spirit knew they couldn't have stood tears without laughter: just as one dear woman was ready to testify, a bug crawled down her dress. . . . For lack of tissue in jungle conditions, they wept into yards of toilet paper, and even that broke them up. . . .

Tears and laughter can't be contrived. You're on the lookout for them—but mostly you ask God to make them happen.

And me in a church pew? If something strikes me funny or if tears well up in my throat, I welcome both as friends. "Hey—the Holy Spirit is here, doing something. Praise God. Keep coming on, Father."

Look for them—in the pulpit, in the pew—those wonderful little extra touches from heaven, laughter and tears.

51

ARE YOUR CHOIR MEMBERS REALLY ALL THERE IN WORSHIP?

Or is it for them a moonlighting job?

You've come through the first half of your church service: the hymns have been sung, the offering's been taken, and the minister is going to preach. Then, every Sunday like clockwork, there's a stealthy exodus—in front of the whole congregation. All those black-robed choir members vanish out a side door.

You whisper to the first-time visitor sitting beside you, "They're going out to attend Sunday School this hour. Some of them teach classes." Or are they going out for breakfast? Or home to bed? And were they *really* in church all through the other service, or aren't they hearing the pastor's sermon at all? You have an uncomfortable sense of maybe being cheated on.

Do you remember that the Israelite singers were full time? It was all they did as service to God. Now I know that many choir members feel a legitimate need for getting in on Sunday School as well—but maybe others need to be challenged to be a "core choir" that stays straight through both (or maybe two out of three) morning services. Then other choir members will add to them for one hour and be in Sunday School the other—but when they're there, they're there for the entire service.

Do you know how beautiful it is not to have any exodus? And the freedom which suddenly opens up? You can put the sermon first, last, or in the middle; the choir is there to be used at any time. Praise the Lord!

It makes a gorgeous difference in the whole service in the feeling of commitment. *We are together, brothers and sisters; we are all together, and we aren't going anywhere else, because our hearts are all here to worship God for this whole hour.*

52

THE MINISTER OF MUSIC UNDERSHEPHERDS HIS CHOIRS

He's got to be at least as much "minister" as "music"

How can you persuade full choirs of people to give themselves to the kind of commitment necessary to do the job? Minister of music or choir director, that's got to be your burden. Prayer is going to have to surround them like a cloud. Let every choir member be a prayer partner with another choir member. In addition, let each choir member have two members of the congregation pledged to support him in prayer every time he sings. Every autumn or new semester the choir people can put quarters into a kitty until they're able to report who their prayer partners and prayer supporters are!

The point is not the mechanics of prayer. The point is that unless the Holy Spirit breathes His life into our music, all it will be is *music*. For that, we can turn on any radio.

Minister of music, are you just *music*, or do you minister? When you look at Susie Schleirmacher, whom do you see? An alto? Or do you see a wife with an overbearing husband, a new home, and an honor-student daughter? Are your people *people* (to be ministered to) or *things* (to be used)?

If at any rehearsal you face four sections of

things, you'll trumpet, "Okay-let's-get-started-we've-got-lotsa-work-to-do-here-tonight-Thanksgiving's-coming-up-and-we-haven't-even-started-on-Christmas-and-I-wonder-if-one-of-you-low-altos-couldn't-sing-tenor?"

But if you face *people,* you'll shepherd them. First you'll take time to worship, to lift them to God. Then you may take time to make sure their hearts are okay; maybe let them share joys and burdens in twos and threes and pray for one another for a little while. When the hurts are eased and the joys expressed and they're getting more deeply involved in one another's lives—

Then begin to sing.

I want to tell you, it will make a difference in the final *sound.*

53

...AND THE CHOIRS SUBMIT TO BEING A FLOCK

Admitting that you need leading isn't easy

Have *you* ever been a choir director? Then you can't imagine all that's involved. Or how hard it is to be a good one!

Eighty percent of a congregation like a similar kind of music. Ten percent want it heavier, and another ten want it lighter. The choir director's burden is to minister to all, so sometimes he moves to the heavy side; then one ten percent will fuss. Other times he moves to the light side; then the opposite ten fuss.

He longs for *the whole service to feed all the people.* Hopefully he understands that services that are all one style, or for all one age group, divide the body. He's got to stretch.

Besides that, he stands under the senior pastor, probably adjacent to a music committee, and over the choir. That's a tight place, man! He's got to squeeze. And he's got to juggle lots of interpersonal relationships, and handle lots of people who have very strong feelings about music—whether they know anything or not.

He's walking a tightrope all the way! Nobody, except the preacher and the youth pastor, gets more criticism.

Choir members, he needs your loyalty, your personal friendship, your compliments, and your pats and hugs and pink fuzzies. Pile 'em on!

And listen: don't give him any back talk. The choir's the one place *he must rule.* A choir director must be a benevolent dictator; otherwise the choir will be in shambles. Even if somebody there knows more about music than he does, forget principles of democracy. Nobody's word must count but his. Choir is a beautiful opportunity to practice submission in the body!

A low point in Israel's history was Judges 21:25, when everybody did that which was right in his own eyes, when there wasn't any king. That's how choirs get to be known as the church's War Department.

Revelation 5:12 expresses the team concept for a choir. It says that the angels sing "in a loud voice"—not "with loud voices." Their praise is all blended into one. Now and then you hear a choir where that is true. Choir, do you know how to make yours like that?

Be prompt to rehearsals.

Don't talk.

Do what you're told.

Never think a rehearsal is too long. Accept extra ones whenever the director says they're necessary.

Become tough, disciplined, uncomplaining.

Ray tells his ministers of music, "Better ten singers who are disciplined, committed, and together than two hundred who are not." Is your choir a trouble spot? Maybe it should be smaller.

When hearts are right, God will increase the musical gift.

54

REBUTTAL TO "WE DON'T HAVE TO PRACTICE. IT'S ONLY A HYMN"

For about fifteen years I was organist for Charles E. Fuller's "Old Fashioned Revival Hour," and then as it became "The Joyful Sound" radio program.

In the studio stood thirty or so singers, many of whom earned their living in full-time professional music.

Rudy Atwood sat at the piano, a world-famous careerist loved by Christians everywhere.

Under Dr. Leland Green's hands we'd sweat out five literal minutes on one completely familiar old line:

"Saviour, more than life to me,
I am clinging, clinging close to Thee."

Dr. Green might say we were relaxing the dotted eighths and sixteenths into triplets and ruining the rhythm. We'd work that through. Then we'd synchronize all the Rs at the end of "more" and the TH of the word "than." We'd pull out "life" a little. We'd dip in volume after "me" without actually breathing. We'd do "clinging, clinging" until we rang like bells.

When all the mechanics were conquered, he might say, "Now add heart." For another five minutes we'd work on that musical line in the dimension of His being more than life—searching for depths of sincerity by "thinking" the message as we sang or played it.

We might spend thirty minutes to put it all together as if we'd never seen it before.

Each week, Dr. Leland Green brought resurrection out from under his hands. Everyone who was ever under that strict training still knows that from the familiar can spring life and renewal and exciting meaning.

55

A SERVICE'S FLOW

"Now, folks—heh, heh—Susie Schleirmacher is going to favor us with an offertory solo"

You're looking at television. Some historic occasion is being brought live to you and in the middle of the screen you're supposed to see the world-famous Mr. So-and-So in the act of doing such-and-such—the most important act of this generation. Unfortunately, a twelve-year-old kid has discovered the camera's live, so there he is, out of focus, in the foreground covering the screen, waving frantically and hamming it up.

And here's church. The act on the screen is the greatest of all: God redeeming man. ("O Lord of Hosts, God of Israel enthroned above the cherubim, you alone are God of all the kingdoms of the earth. . . .")

But unfortunately, all we can see is George—hearty, folksy, grinning George, "Thank you, choir, for that fantastic number, yessir, you folks musta really practiced that one, and now everybody turn to hymn 22 and let's really hear you sing it like you mean it, yessir, that's what we're all here for, so let's just let it all out, are you ready on the first word. . . ."

The *Los Angeles Times* writer Charles Champlin says, "In art, *less is more.* What is true can always be simply said." (Would you agree that a worship service is man's highest art form?)

"Less is more!" Job to God: "I lay my hand upon my mouth in silence. I have said too much already" (40:4,5, *TLB*).

"Less is more!" Pastor, please read through the chapters in this book for your other staffers, and tell them to read your chapters. (All of you have to melt together into the same flavor!) In chapter 49 on classical organ literature there are these sentences: "Never play a single note without meaning. . . . To the extent that you put in filler which is excelsior and sawdust, to that extent your people will be tempted to grow dull and ho-hum as you play."

This is just as true of speaking. Now, perhaps God has made you a hearty and verbose person. He works through personalities so don't think you suddenly have to become Austere Arthur.

But look at your printed order of worship. There's no reason to repeat orally what's already before their eyes. If the transition needs music, let the organ bridge it meaningfully (or a soloist, or the choir, or whatever). If the need of the moment is the spoken word, don't duplicate the printed page, but supplement it. Call attention to the meaning of what's happening; let someone else read a verse of related Scripture, or a quotation, or—

Once, just before our choir was going to sing about Christ's second coming to earth, Ray had two laymen read current newspaper headlines back and forth for about one minute—fulfillments of prophecy as a buildup to the fantastic news that He's coming!

Think about your service's flow. Your subject

matter is so tremendous that maybe your biggest need is to prune and let the subject matter show!
   "Less is more."

56

ANNOUNCEMENTS

Clear your brain, here comes a new metaphor

/ The worship service is a fire you're feeding. And the announcement time is a filled squirt gun.

"Next Tuesday morning the ladies will gather at ten o'clock in the parlor to quilt. . ." Psss! One of the flames is shot out.

"If there are any volunteers to help in the Daily Vacation Bible School starting tomorrow morning, would you please see Rachel McGruder. . ." Pow! Another part of the fire goes cold.

A few more and you may be hunting for matches again.

Announcements are the only part of a service which, by their very nature, edify nobody. They in no way build up the Body or introduce unbelievers to the Saviour. Hearts do not beat faster over announcements.

Therefore, here are a few suggested rules:

1. Announcements should not repeat what is already in the bulletin. Americans are something like ninety-seven percent literate. Announcements are what bulletins were invented for.

2. Announcements should not pertain to only a part of the congregation (a committee, the young people, the women, etc.). A worship service is a

togetherness experience. Don't lessen that by excluding large segments of people, not even for sixty seconds.

Let the special groups learn to rely on the bulletin, on bulletin inserts, on posters around the church campus, on the mails, on telephones, etc. But don't let them intrude into worship.

3. Never announce appeals for volunteers for anything (not in the bulletin, either). A church never has to whine and plead. The Holy Spirit is committed to giving gifts to His church which will abundantly fill every need. (Obviously, if He doesn't supply a particular gift for *your* church, He must not consider this a need.) Relying on His promise, those concerned can pray in private for the right ones to come forward and volunteer. Or they can pray for wisdom to discern gifts in their fellow believers and then ask qualified people. Even the smallest churches can believe God!

Can you put away your squirt gun entirely? Happy fire-tending.

57

A WORSHIP SERVICE REALLY CAN BE WORSHIP

That pew can become holy ground

"I've never adored the Lord before," said a long-time Christian at a conference recently. There were tears in her eyes. "I've attended worship services all my life, but I never worshiped until today."

Christian, it's up to you, when you come to church, to worship. Nobody can do it for you. All those helps—hymns, prayers, sermons—lead you to the water, but they can't make you drink.

You, personally, must lift your heart to God. *"How can I please you today, Father?"*

Surely by first confessing your sins. You are unworthy to come into His presence! In Acts 3:19 Peter said so earnestly, not to heathen, but to God's people: "Repent, then, and turn to God, so that your sins may be wiped out, that times of refreshing may come from the Lord."

Be specific: *"Father, I'm so sorry that this morning I blew my lid; so-and-so was my fault."*

Does this bring to mind an apology you owe somebody? Could you even slip out of your pew and make it right before church begins? Matthew 5:23,24: "Therefore, if you are offering your gift at the altar and there remember that your brother has something against you, leave your gift there in front of the altar. First go and be reconciled to your brother; then come and offer your gift."

Right on! Leave your offering envelope with an usher just in case the apology takes longer and you don't get back!

And what's worship all about? It's admiring God. Do you do that? Worship is a muscle that is so little used, most of us don't know how. Tell God how wonderful He is by every fresh, innovative way you can.

If you happen to ask a group of Christians in a prayer meeting to offer God worship, they'll probably turn it into thanksgiving: "Thank you, Lord, for being so kind to me . . ." and they've turned the spotlight onto themselves again.

How about adoration the way Solomon's Song of Songs does it? "You are beautiful. . . . Like a lily among thorns . . . a sachet of myrrh . . ."

Tell God, "Oh, my Father, you are . . ." and fill in the blank! Discipline your concentration on who He is and what He does. Not necessarily what He does for *you* (see how God describes Himself in Job 38-41), just what He does, in His matchless wisdom and power.

Think of adjectives that describe Him. Nouns that describe Him. Maybe go through the alphabet, an initial for each.

Concentrate on God—stretch your mind. Adore Him.

Lord, this church service is for you. I'm here to give you pleasure.

58

SACRAMENTS ARE SPECIAL

Be sure you keep them that way

There are two rituals for believers that have to do with worship and that are especially holy and set apart. They have been for two thousand years.

But suddenly in this day, when the fabric of our living is becoming stretched, frayed, and torn, these two sacraments have sometimes been snatched loose and let float around free. It's a little scary. You need to think about them.

The two rituals are water baptism and the Lord's Supper. And they're called *sacraments* because that means they're very sacred. They're to be set apart from all common uses for a sacred use, and they've usually been observed through the centuries in connection with the gathering of believers for worship.

Anybody can jump into a bathtub and take a bath. Anybody who swims can jump into a pool or ocean under safe conditions. What's so special and different about baptism?

In the Word of God, baptism was apparently a once-in-a-lifetime experience. Whether John's baptisms of people flocking to him in the desert for the forgiveness of their sins (Mark 1:4,5), or Jesus' disciples' baptisms of new adherents to the Kingdom (John 4:1,2; Matt. 28:18-20; Acts 2:41; etc.)—the inference is that it was a once-for-all ritual, symbolizing identification with Christ instead of the world.

The eunuch's baptism at conversion (Acts 8:27-39) and the fact that Paul could name the converts he'd baptized (1 Cor. 1:14-16) both seem to add confirmation. They infer, "Baptism is big deal, people! Be careful of it."

Through succeeding centuries, Christians differed on just how to baptize, so you had a few people saying, "It wasn't done right the first time; let's do it again." Of this the church at large has been tolerant, but was still careful to see that the applicant was truly qualified, that the occasion was appropriate, that records were kept, and that all was done reverently and in the spirit of a true "sacrament."

In this generation, suddenly Christians are exclaiming, "Praise the Lord! I feel wonderful! I do believe I'm having some new experience!" and they jump into somebody's swimming pool and have themselves easy-does-it-baptisms. Anybody does the baptizing; it may be the first time or the fifth— who cares? And there is no responsible notifying of a pastor or a local Body to follow up with nurture and instruction and love.

Frankly, it makes me nervous. (Signed, Anne Ortlund.)

I feel equally uneasy about sudden ordinations, reordinations, ordinations done by just anybody, et cetera. But that's another story.

The other sacrament connected with worship is the Lord's Supper—and light handling of that scares me even more, because God's restrictions and penalties connected with it are so severe.

Until recently, churches decided whether to

observe Communion weekly, monthly, quarterly, or whatever. How they decided was Big Deal to them and carefully prayed over. And for two thousand years only those with recognized ordinations—on whose heads the hands of the fathers had placed approval after much training and prayerful consideration of their quality of personal life—only they were qualified either to baptize or to administer Communion.

Suddenly everybody's doin' it! Jump into the act; it's great for camps and retreats, weddings, ladies' missionary meetings, even home parties. When you want to "change moods," lower the lights and serve Communion. When you want to end a program on a "spiritual" note, it's just the ticket.

Now, I understand that the proliferation of the observances of both these sacraments has come with the proliferation of believers who love to celebrate their precious experiences in Him. (What a wonderful day we live in!) And personally, I've only participated in home Communions that were very reverent and special.

But just for the record, what do God's instructions seem to be? First Corinthians 11:17-34 is the classic how-to passage on Communion. It seems to be saying that ordinary meals are to happen at home (vv. 22 and 34), and Communion is to happen when believers come together to worship (vv. 20, 33, 34).

And Communion is so powerful that if it's mishandled it makes Christians either sicken or die (vv. 27-30). So there's wisdom in its usually being a total-church function. It gives more control; it's more apt to be prayed over, thought through, and the celebrants thoroughly prepared for it.

Have a heart, people! Don't make me nervous! If

you're contemplating a slightly off-key baptism or Communion, why don't you say, "Well, maybe the Lord wouldn't mind, but if it will make Anne Ortlund feel better, let's not."

I'll thank you in heaven.

Honest.

———————————

P.S. Did you ever have a preparation meeting Thursday or Friday evening before Sunday Communion, just for prayer and the searching of hearts? It's wonderful.

AN ALTERNATIVE TO CHURCHGOING

You don't *have* to sit through a worship service. . .

Instead, select a secluded room where you can take a brother or a sister and go pray through the service. Pray with one eye on the clock:

Pray for the ushers as they're seating the people

Pray for a great spirit of anticipation over the congregation

Pray for the organist in his prelude

Pray for the latecomers

For the choir

The other up-fronters

The pastoral prayer

The hymns

The anthem

The visitors, the seekers, the troubled. . . .

Pray back and forth in conversational prayer straight through the service, sermon and all.

The word will spread; the group may grow; the service will greatly gain in power—so will the sermon.

They say that when Charles Spurgeon preached, there were 500 in the basement praying for him.

No wonder he was some preacher.

THAT EXCITING SCRIPTURE READING

Who knows—maybe it will punch a hole in the sky

When our family lived in England a few years ago we often tramped around the wonderful old churches there. I remember particularly one little country church, many centuries old, with its Gothic proportions and its damp, mossy stone. . ., this church had a surprise for us.

Here was the big front door for everyone to go in. Well, no, not everyone. Over to the left was a slot in the outside wall like a letter drop. It was called the "lepers' squint"! Oh, dear God, couldn't all your children go into church?

No, the ones with leprosy huddled around the slot in the wall and took turns peering through. How precious each turn must have been! One leper might get in on five percent of the second hymn, thirty-five percent of the offering being taken; then it was time to move over.

Let's try it over his left shoulder; maybe I can see a bit more. But that's the end of the slot; let's try the right. Nope, somebody else got there first. What was that last sentence? What did he say? Bless their hearts, what a way to worship God.

You're wondering what this story has to do

with Scripture reading in church. Stick with me; it will fit soon.

Think about the whole universe—all of creation—every atom of it jammed, crammed with wisdom, morality, beauty, joy. The morning stars sing together. One moment of time stands shoulder to shoulder with the next moment for a duet. Righteousness, space, truth, and time superimpose, synchronize, flow. How can we figure it? How can our heads get it all together?

God chooses for now to give us just a few brief clues: enough to know we must accept and love and worship Jesus Christ—plus only a few other mouth-watering glimpses into what the whole thing is about.

And all the clues, all the glimpses are in His one Book. His "lepers' squint"!

———————

Now think about it. All Christ's people gather together on a Sunday morning, and this Book is going to be read from.

(Oh, minister! Study it in advance. Underline key words for emphasis. Practice it out loud.)

In the special Holy Spirit atmosphere of Jesus' presence among His gathered people, here comes the high point of the service: we're going to squint through those brief, few words at God's Everything.

People, all of us, listen! *What's God saying? What did He mean by that last sentence? Don't go so fast, Pastor; we're not getting it.*

God!

Vastness is behind your words! Seas crashing, solar systems roaring,—and the Cross, the Cross!

Read it over, Pastor. What was that again?

61

HOW NOT TO LISTEN TO A SERMON

(with your red pencil ready)

Here's a typical teenager listening to negative criticism from his mother. His response is, "How I thank you for that! I really needed it and I love you for telling me." Right?

Wrong. Almost a hundred times out of a hundred his reaction will be, "Why should I take this from you? You're not so perfect yourself. How come you always. . ." and the bell has sounded for the boxing match to begin. Rebuke has bred rebuke!

A preacher is a substitute parent. He's got one of the world's toughest jobs. All his life he must handle the Scriptures in "teaching, rebuking, correcting, and training in righteousness" (2 Tim. 3:16). Are most listeners mature enough to say, "I love that man for pointing out my flaws"? No way.

So even unconsciously their defense mechanisms take over, and rebuke breeds rebuke. They can't usually say, "The pastor was wrong about my greed or my selfishness," so they say instead:

1. "He preaches too long."
2. "His voice is too high."
3. "He waves his hands too much."
4. (If he tells too many stories) "His sermons

aren't biblical enough."

5. (Or if he doesn't tell enough stories) "His sermons aren't practical enough."

6. "He's too intellectual."

7. "He's too simplistic."

8. "He's too old for us."

9. "He's too young for us."

Or they cut him down to size by his Monday-to-Saturday role:

10. "He's not a strong enough leader."

11. (Or if he's a strong leader) "He's power-hungry."

12. (If he's a lover of people) "He doesn't study enough."

13. (Or if he's a lover of study) "He's not available enough."

With many people he can't win. Jesus, the model Preacher, had the same complaint: "John the Baptist came neither eating bread nor drinking wine, and you say, 'He has a demon.' The Son of Man came eating and drinking, and you say, 'Here is a glutton and a drunkard'" (Luke 7:33,34).

You've heard the term "red pencil mentality," and it describes the attitude of many a churchgoer. He imagines his pew to be the judgment seat of God, and as soon as he takes his place in it he has his red pencil ready. Nothing escapes his critiquing: the ushers were slow at one point; the assistant pastor goofed on two words in the Scripture reading; the pastor shouldn't have mentioned so-and-so; the choir was better than usual but the choice of anthem was a tad heavy . . .

How the spirit of evaluation slips out in even well-meaning words to pastors like, "Boy, you get better every week!"

The pastor's probably tempted to pump his

hand and say, "And I want to tell you, you sure are getting better at listening than you used to be. Maybe some day I'll even see some change in your behavior!"

But that's reactionary—and that is forever a no-no for every pastor. Maybe his flock has bugged him all week. Nevertheless, it's not fair for him to get in the last word by blasting them in his sermon. Every hostility shows in the pulpit. And without love his message is nothing—a mere tinkling cymbal.

A wise parent combines rebuke and exhortation with compliments and words of loving reassurance. So does a wise pastor!

Recently I visited a church where a fussing pastor is breeding a fussing congregation. Everybody's losing. Ray had breakfast with the fellow and urged him to pray for every member every week, straight through his membership roll over and over, asking God to give him love for each one.

Still, people, "the burden of the Lord" is heavy enough on the back of any pastor without throwing on more lead weights. Unchecked, the red pencil mentality can add to the statistics of one more pastor who divorces his wife, has a nervous breakdown, or at the very least, changes to selling insurance.

62

A SERMON DOESN'T HAVE TO BE ALL AT ONCE

Teaching situations need all the ingenuity they can get

I'd spoken at a Friday-Saturday retreat for the women of Fourth Presbyterian Church in Washington, D.C. On Sunday I slipped into a pew to worship there. (That's a lively, strategic, cleansing place.) In the evening service the former pastor, Dr. Richard Halverson, preached half his sermon. Then he sat down and we stood up and sang a while. Then we sat down and he stood up and finished his sermon.

Why not? "The mind can absorb only as much as the seat can endure."

Lake Avenue Church once put together Romans 8 and Bach (selections from his cantata *Jesu, Priceless Treasure*) for its morning service. After a few preliminaries Dr. Bruce Leafblad, our minister of music at the time, whose heart beat as Ray's and who worked hand-in-glove with him, explained that our worship that morning would be divided into three parts—three sections of the eighth chapter of Romans. The sections were printed complete in the Order of Worship.

First Ray preached for about ten minutes on the first section, then the choir sang it. Then Ray preached on the second section, and the choir sang that. Then section three—preached and then sung. Benediction.

Instruction, inspiration, and beauty!

63

PREACHING

It's outside of everybody, even the preacher

Old Professor Wheeler was the end of an era at Princeton Seminary. He had coached the Barrymores in voice, and when he taught his seminarians to preach, he taught them to *preach*.

After his day, all over the nation the theory came into vogue that preachers were to "share," to get down on the level of their listeners and not come across like some big authority.

Praise the Lord my young husband got in on the end of Prof Wheeler. I can see Ray yet in our little student apartment making his stomach muscles go in and out and practicing bringing his voice up from some unknown depths so he could "project." Did he practice projecting!

First to people fifteen feet away: "Strike the flagstaff deep, sir knight!"

Then to people fifty feet away: "Scatter flowers, fair maids!"

Then to people in the back of some top balcony: "Ho, gunners! Fire a loud salute!"

And then to an imaginary audience across the length of a football field (his shirt really leaving and meeting his belt buckle, and his voice a deep

Shakespearean roar), "Ho, gallants! Draw—your—blades!"

For the first few years Ray preached, every Sunday morning early he was still barking, "Ho! ho!" around the house, as he worked his stomach muscles and thought about where to place his voice so he could project.

The reason? Prof Wheeler's theory was that the preacher *should* come across like a big authority. Why? Not because he is anything in himself, but because his message is the Word of God.

The secret of preaching is for the man to divorce himself from his message. With all the authority of an Old Testament prophet he's to thunder, "Thus saith the Lord!" No "sharing." No apologies.

Then with utter openness and honesty he's to say, "I need this too. . . . Nobody needs this Word more than I. . . . God had to deal with me this morning before I could preach this to you. . . ."

A man who loses confidence in the Word of God is one who has to "share." His only offering is his own opinion to be considered along with other equally valid opinions. He'd better keep his voice folksy and apologetic—because he may be wrong and he doesn't want to appear perfect, as if he were Mr. Know-It-All.

After all, he doesn't want to *preach at them*. . . .

Have you noticed lately, as authority figures have lost stature, that the word *preach* has gotten bad connotations? "I don't want to sound preachy, but. . ."; "Now, I'm not trying to *preach* to you. . ."

But 1 Corinthians 1 says that to us who are being saved, preaching is the power of God unto salvation.

Preach is a fabulous word. Preaching is full of

glory and mystery. Many of the shining moments in Christendom's history have come as the church of Christ sat under the preaching of the Word of God.

Do you disagree that the man must be divorced from his message?

In comic strips a person stands below and his words are printed in a balloon up above.

There you've got it!

The preacher below is, in himself, totally inadequate and totally unworthy. He's got to let the people know he's not the perfect embodiment of the words in that balloon above him. But if that balloon is the preaching of the cross, if it's the power of God unto salvation—

In that case—whisper it, shout it, pound it home, take it in, absorb it, treasure it, pass it on, live it out—preacher and people alike.

William Nagenda was a preacher from the heart of Africa. He stood in our pulpit one Sunday morning, tiny and shiny black, and began in his high-pitched voice, "I said to the Lord, 'O Lord, what shall I tell this people? I feel so dry.' And the Lord said, 'Tell them you are dry.' "

What happened? An electric current of sympathy for William swept through the congregation. (Who hasn't felt dry?) We all began to pray—not for a fabulous African preacher who didn't need any help and who was vulnerable for all judgmental and critical comparisons, but for a small, frail new friend who had to speak when he felt dry. His honesty had disarmed us and won us.

William Nagenda preached long and vigorously, with such conviction and power that few of us will ever forget it. The frail man below had separated himself from the balloon above. The Word of God was freed to be full of power and authority.

Without that separation a preacher has two choices. He can shout and swagger, hide his personal failures, cultivate admirers, and become a fraud. Or he can admit his humanness, try to be just "one of the boys," and share his uncertainty as a blind man leading the blind.

There is another alternative: "I'm not much, but, friends, what I have to say is life or death. I need it. You need it. Let's receive it together. 'O earth, earth, earth, hear the Word of the Lord!' "

———————

There's just one requirement: you'd better study the Book all week long. Make sure that in the balloon there's only God's Word, and not yours.

64

HOW TO LISTEN TO A SERMON
Just listen for God

Is your church experience really one-on-one with God? Are you bowed low before Him alone— to admire Him, tell Him of your love, ask forgiveness, get directions? Then everything, from the first moment of the prelude until you're out the door again, is His aggressive confrontation of you. Then you can name the little spot where you sat *Peniel* (Gen. 32:30), because you've been face to face with God.

The hymn words are just for you. The Scripture reading is to call you up short on something, or comfort you, or challenge you. The experiences of your past week were all shaped to prepare you for this moment, and everything—the combination of people, the order of the service, even the expressions on each face—everything is created by God for His personal confrontation of you.

The sermon is for that. The point is *you must internalize it.* As long as your center of attention is outside yourself—other people, the building, the preacher, or even the sermon—you're not hearing with the inner ear.

Take the message within yourself. Picture it within your own body. How is it changing *your heart, your life*? Whether you're a mature believer or a new baby Christian, the Holy Spirit is grading the material as it passes into your ears *just for you.*

Preaching hasn't become preaching, as far as you personally are concerned, until you have learned the difficult, rigorous habit of internalizing it.

Is the sermon a poor one? Through its poverty God is saying to you something profound! Tuck away that red pencil with embarrassed apologies to Him, and *listen to Him.*

Maybe He will come to you as He did to John. His voice will be like the sound of rushing waters, and out of His mouth will come a sharp double-edged sword (Rev. 1:15,16)! What a traumatic experience! Let Him cut you. The wounds will heal powerfully. (Who knows—His subsequent instructions may be as to John: "Write what you have seen"!)

He may confront you with teaching, as He did Ezekiel, unrolling a scroll before you and saying, "Son of man,. . .eat this scroll." And you eat it, and it tastes sweet as honey in your mouth (Ezek. 2:9–3:3).

He may come to you with a commission, as to Isaiah: "Whom shall I send? And who will go for us?. . . Go and tell this people . . ." (Isa. 6:8,9).

However He comes, He will come. Wait for His Word. In everything you hear be eager for it, search for it.

In a Spirit-filled service everything may be His powerful speaking to You! In a thin service He may speak through one snatch of word or phrase. Have your pen ready (not your red pencil; it's gone),

your note-taking pen and notebook, to capture
every word that He's telling you.
    And remember! Internalize it.

65

WHAT MAKES A SERMON BIBLICAL?

One of the reasons so many Christians have their red pencils ready to whip out, I think, is that everybody has his own idea of what kind of sermon is the Real Thing.

"It mentions the Lord's name a lot." Well, the whole book of Esther never does; think about it.

"It mentions the blood." Galatians doesn't; Philippians doesn't; 1 and 2 Thessalonians do not, nor 1 and 2 Timothy, nor Titus, nor Philemon. . . . Few of the New Testament Epistles do.

Now when you read the whole sweep of Scriptures from beginning to end, they are obsessed with God! And the theme of the blood goes from Genesis to Revelation. But don't pounce on a preacher after one sermon, or six. Give him a year!

"A truly biblical sermon is expository, verse by verse." How can this be the most biblical when there is not one expository sermon in the Bible itself? By Jesus' day the whole Old Testament Scriptures were complete, but it's never recorded that He took a section and preached it verse by verse. Peter's sermon in Acts 2 was on a subject, the resurrection, with quotations from Joel and the Psalms. Stephen's sermon in Acts 7 was a historical survey.

My husband's usual style is expository, and I love it—but Billy Graham's powerful style often is not. And God forbid that we should "touch the Lord's anointed" in criticism!

People, we're not so smart. Let's sit humbly in our seats and let the Lord speak to us.

66

TURNING AWAY FROM THE MIRROR

Take a look at James 1:22-25 for the picture

Somewhere I heard the story of the fellow who overslept and came rushing up the steps of the church just as another fellow was coming out.

"Is the sermon over?" he puffed.

"No, it's just beginning," was the answer. "Now we're going out to do it."

Response is the name of the game. The first ten minutes after a sermon are crucial to whether the seed falls on good ground and takes root and changes lives, or whether birds immediately pick it up and fly off forever.

What are your people going to *do* as a result of what they've *heard*?

This burden is no doubt what gave birth to the "invitation." An invitation gets unbelievably wearisome if it's the only thing a pastor knows to do Sunday after identical Sunday. It's a great device if used sparingly along with many other techniques.

Once when Ray preached on forgiveness he asked us to write down on paper our individual "worst sins." He waited in quiet as we thought and wrote. Then he had us write "1 John 1:9" across the face of the whole list, and tear up our papers.

Pastor, perhaps you should ask your flock to write down what they individually resolve to do the coming week, to act on the challenge of God from the sermon.

Perhaps you should ask each one to vow a vow to God to be accomplished by some future date, say three months or six months hence. The church keeps the cards and mails them back on D-date. Each person can check to see if he reached his goal.

Suppose you're exhorting your flock to be encouragers. Then suggest that everyone seek out one person after the service to whom he'll say, "I love you," "I appreciate you," or "I'm thankful you did so-and-so." Believe me, visitors would stand around thrilled at watching such a display of love. They won't feel left out—just maybe jealous of such a fellowship.

Or, instead, have them fill out blank cards which have been placed in the pew racks—writing words of love to one brother or sister—which they hand on personally after the service or put in the mail.

Occasionally you might ask them to hold hands and pray for the one on their right and then the one on their left: that God will help them to obey what God suggested to them in the sermon.

Once in a while you might ask them to raise their hands or stand—to receive Christ for the first time or to respond to some Christian challenge.

Once in another while perhaps you'll ask them to step right out of their seats and come forward (no secret handraising first lest they feel trapped into some scheme). Here an altar rail is a wonderful help. If your church has steps across the front they accomplish the same thing. For the physical body to kneel publicly makes a deep impression on others' hearts!

A while back, after such an experience, a doctor's beautiful wife wrote Ray, "A miracle happened in my life on Sunday, and I want to share it with you. I have been a Christian for a long time, but until Sunday I have never felt cleansed. I needed to physically lay all my sins on the altar and *accept* His forgiveness."

The Israelite of old personally laid his hand on the head of a sacrificial animal.

Pastor, how long will you keep your people merely listeners, with no choice of action after hearing God's Word but to file out to the tune of a postlude?

67

THE CONCLUSION OF THE SERVICE

It's time to go. What a shame.

This is the time to squeeze out the last juices so that the taste lingers in our mouths.

This is the time to release the perfume that follows us out the door and home.

What's been happening? Continue it.

Did the sermon end full of high victory? Think in terms of a closing hymn and benediction that are short blasts of triumph. Then let the organ sock it to them, fortissimo. Watch people walk out grinning from ear to ear.

Did the sermon end thoughtfully, quietly? There's the cue for minister and organist.

Was the final hymn particularly special? Then why should the choir do their planned choral amen? Instead, the minister of music can point to the final verse of the hymn and they can tenderly repeat it. Then, organist, never mind what the bulletin says your postlude is. Continue that hymn, or play another one on a related subject as the people go.

Sometimes have the choir sing the people out. Sometimes have the people sing themselves out.

Keep the theme going somehow right out the door.

Never a dull moment.

Make them sorry it's over—and ready to come back for more.

68

IT'S STILL DIALOGUE TIME

The congregation's got the last word

The service is over and you're heading out.

The pastor, if he's any kind of preacher at all, is drained of adrenalin. He's at the door. He has stripped himself of everything he has for the congregation's sake, and there he stands, vulnerable, chilly, and trembling, in his birthday suit!!

If you pass him by, he's dead. It's a lonely moment, and he needs your response. (If he thinks he preached a monologue he'll have bad dreams tonight.)

Now there's a line of people behind you, so don't take too long. Suddenly everyone is starving, including the preacher.

Don't make some remark about the latest Dodger score; that's unreal! He has spoken to you of heaven and eternity.

Plan your words to be brief, tender, lifting:

"Well, I've got a lot to work on this week."

"I'm going to study that third point some more."

"Wow! What a thought in that last verse!"

"Well, God socked it to me again."

"Thank you, my friend; I needed that."

How about the most lifting words of all—"Pas-

tor, we'd like to introduce our neighbors. . . ."
   That'll keep him encouraged for six whole days.

69

AFTER THE POSTLUDE

Everything depends on the Monday-to-Saturday span

The sons of Levi were born into their work. They were enmeshed in worship, as their ancestors had been and as their descendants would be.

We're not like that, but just the same, church up-fronters can't minister heaven to people on Sunday, pick up a paycheck, and live like a child of hell the rest of the week.

To quote the various translations of Romans 6:2, "God forbid." "By no means." "Of course not." "No, no!" "Not at all!" "Never!" "Certainly not!" "What a ghastly thought!"

Consider yourself this way, church musician: you don't "have a church job"; you are a church choir director, organist, or whatever. That's a continuing ministry for which you need to be a continuing kind of person. (Somehow the pastor's role is more settled; he is the pastor, and that's that. He's *always* the pastor. That's why you can feel free to phone him at two in the morning.)

Friend organist, let's go a step further. Don't be known to the people as just an organist; be known as a godly person. Music isn't where it's at: *God* is where it's at! Music is a great vehicle, but it's only a vehicle, a carrier.

I could improvise on this theme for a long time. No organ number can forgive your sins, graft you into the Body of Christ, and promise you an eternal inheritance. There are no fruits of a fugue or a passacaglia, only the fruits of the Spirit. You can be a sour old man or woman behind that instrument.

What am I trying to say?

Well, of course during the week you'll give yourself to hours of hard work in practice; there's no other way. But don't make music your escape. Come out from behind that console, friend, and get where the action is.

Be involved in non-musical activities in the church: get into a small group for Bible study and prayer.

Give yourself away. What can you do to make others happy?

Share your faith with that doubting neighbor. Connect him up with somebody he can sit with in church.

Develop relationships! Love your pastor. Thank God for your choir director. (He's your boss too, you know.) Be on the team; be loyal. Don't even listen to hostile criticism; give your brothers and sisters on the church staff dignity and honor, "because of their work" (1 Thess. 5:13).

Be a Barnabas, an encourager. Instead of expecting people to come to the organ to compliment you, be the aggressor. Thank the soloist; encourage the choir; express your appreciation to the choir director, the preacher, and others who serve.

I hate to admit it, but sometimes ministers need to be faced with this Monday-to-Saturday bit too. Their profession becomes a game they play, a mask they put on.

How Ray and I shuddered when, early in our ministry, a neighboring pastor spent his day off with us and said it sure was fun to get away from his church people for a change so he could relax and cuss and be himself. Poor, poor man.

And I'll never forget the minister's wife whose husband was just about to retire, and she gleefully side-mouthed to me, "I've almost drunk my last damn cup of tea!" Poor, poor woman. What a tragedy. What a waste.

Oh, the exhilaration of being for real! Not of being perfect, but of walking before God! Of ministering before Him, being with others before Him, being alone before Him, working before Him, playing hilariously before Him, eating-sleeping-breathing before Him, with Him, in Him!

Alleluia!

Oh, my Father, what a life!

I stretch out my soul before you and say, "Thanks, thanks, thanks. You're so—SPLENDID!"

70

SUPPOSE IT REALLY HAPPENS

After all the blood, sweat, and tears, God comes.

He descends over all the people like a canopy and together you become aware that you're in a new dimension. You've broken into glory!

I can't describe how it will be for you. It will be different than when He comes to any other group of believers. You will all look like the same old friends to one another, and yet you'll all be different.

There will be a new identification with some of those heavenly scenes in the book of Revelation. Praise will be there, and joy, and new words from familiar lips.

At that moment all the up-fronters need to remember one of Dr. Tozer's stories.

It's the first Palm Sunday, and here comes Jesus riding into Jerusalem on a donkey. The crowds begin to shout "Hosanna! Hosanna!" The old donkey pricks up his ears. Some in the crowd throw their coats in the road; others spread out palm branches.

"Well!" says the donkey, switching a fly off a mange patch. "I had no idea they really appreciated me like this! Listen to those hosannas, would you. I must really be something!"

Friends, if anybody comes around after the service saying, "Wow! That was terrific!"—they're not actually saying hosanna to *you*.

All you did was bring Jesus to them.

OTHER GOOD READING FROM REGAL BOOKS